FULLY ALIVE

Richard E. Myers Lectures
Presented by University Baptist Church, Charlottesville
REV. DR. MATTHEW A. TENNANT, EDITOR

Fully Alive

The Apocalyptic Humanism of Karl Barth

Stanley Hauerwas

UNIVERSITY OF VIRGINIA PRESS
Charlottesville and London

First published 2022

1 3 5 7 9 8 6 4 2

Library of Congress Cataloging-in-Publication Data

Names: Hauerwas, Stanley, author.
Title: Fully alive : the apocalyptic humanism of Karl Barth / Stanley Hauerwas.
Description: Charlottesville : University of Virginia Press, 2022. | Series: Richard R. Myers
lectures | Includes bibliographical references and index.
Identifiers: LCCN 2021030572 (print) | LCCN 2021030573 (ebook) | ISBN 9780813947037
(hardcover) | ISBN 9780813947044 (ebook)
Subjects: LCSH: Barth, Karl, 1886–1968. | Barth, Karl, 1886–1968—Influence. | Theology. |
Christian humanism.
Classification: LCC BX4827.B3 H38 2022 (print) | LCC BX4827.B3 (ebook) |
DDC 230/.044092—dc23
LC record available at https://lccn.loc.gov/2021030572
LC ebook record available at https://lccn.loc.gov/2021030573

To Jim and Marcia May Childress

CONTENTS

Preface   *ix*

Introduction   1

1 | The Christian Message in the World Today   9

2 | The Christian Message, the Work of Theology,
    and the New Humanism   23

3 | The Church and Civil Society   39

4 | Reinhold Niebuhr: An Insightful Theologian   53

5 | Karl Barth and Reinhold Niebuhr: Their Differences Matter   64

6 | God and Alasdair MacIntyre: With a Nod to Barth   81

7 | Wounded: The Church and Pastoral Care   100

8 | The Church in Asia: A Barthian Meditation   117

9 | Race: Fifty Years Later   135

10 | To Be Befriended: A Meditation on Friendship
     and the Disabled   152

Afterword: Advice to Christian Theologians   *165*

Appendix: On Writing Theology   *171*

Notes   *179*

Index   *193*

Contents

viii

PREFACE

My life is made possible by gifts from friends, including the gift of friendship itself. I have written this book under the influence of many friends. I am particularly indebted to Greg Jones, Jonathan Tran, Brian Brock, Sam Wells, and Natalie Carnes. The lectures using Barth were originally delivered at Regent College in Vancouver. I am particularly indebted to Jens Zimmerman's responses as I prepared the lectures. In return, the best thing I can do is recommend his fine book *Dietrich Bonhoeffer's Christian Humanism*. I am grateful to President Jeff Greenman's wonderful hospitality during my stay at Regent. I am equally indebted to Rev. Matthew Tennant's care of me when I delivered the Myers Lectures at University Baptist in Charlottesville, Virginia. Reverend Tennant proved to be an engaging theological interlocutor.

I have called some of my past publications "kitchen sink books." I used that description to acknowledge that the chapters in the book are only loosely interrelated. This is not a kitchen sink book. These essays and lectures are my attempt to show the power of Barth's theology. Though the lectures were given in quite diverse settings—Japan, South Bend, Dallas—I think the reader will find that, taken together, they are more than the sum of their parts.

Finally, I am again in Carole Taylor's debt for turning these collected lectures and essays into a book. After many years of making me better than I am, Carole has now finished her Th.D. in theology, and she is doing theology with a vitality that will be lasting.

This is my last book as a faculty member of Duke Divinity School. I owe that school a great deal. I am humbled and honored to have been a part of its mission of forming ministers of Christ's gospel. In so doing, I hope I have served Christ's church well.

Thanks,
Stanley Hauerwas

FULLY ALIVE

INTRODUCTION

And then everything changed. I had conceived and put this book together before the outbreak of the virus. The virus, however, seems to make life prior to it become an unreal reality. We, and that "we" means everybody, had not experienced an illness which seemed to have no cure and is not easily controlled. If ever there was an apocalyptic moment, this seems to be it. The wish for a new normal betrays the assumption that we knew what the normal was prior to the pandemic.

This raises the question of whether I should bother publishing this book. If we now live in a new world, is it not the case that the subjects that are central to this book are simply no longer relevant? I think that not to be the case for no other reason than that Karl Barth is the central figure in this book. If there has ever been an apocalyptic theologian, Barth surely deserves that description. That is not only because he lived through an apocalyptic time but also because he saw the world as forever changed by a Galilean peasant.

It is the burden of this book to show that Barth's radical theological perspective is not incompatible with a deep humanism. Just as the virus in many ways reveals what has always been the case, that is, when all is said and done, we are all going to be dead, so Barth's engagements with the challenges of his day can help us see what it means for us to be human beings. I hope to show that his work can be read as a training manual that can help us to maintain our humanity in a world in crisis.

This book was also conceived and written before Jennifer Herdt's *Forming Humanity: Redeeming the German Bildung Tradition* had been published.[1] In her book, Herdt takes on the task of redeeming the "Bildung" tradition even though the major figures in that movement— Kant, Herder, Humboldt, Schiller, Goethe, and Hegel—took a very critical stance toward Christianity in the name of recovering a robust humanism. Herdt argues, however, that their work can be appropriated as aids in the ongoing project of formulating a Christian humanism for our day. In fact, she thinks that "redeeming" work was begun by the theologian often identified as the enemy of the Bildung tradition, that is, Karl Barth.

Herdt recognizes that most would not count Barth as an advocate of such a renewed humanism. It is true that the high humanism of liberal theology was the enemy for Barth. Barth had no use for those theologies that put a transcendent humanity at the center of existence. Yet Herdt, drawing on Barth's great book *Protestant Thought: From Rousseau to Ritschl*, argues that "in a certain sense" Barth stood within the Bildung tradition just to the extent he saw that culture "is a task, the task of the realization of humanity, conceived of in part as the synthesis of a series of oppositions" that can only be united through an encounter with God.[2] To be a human being, which is not a given but a task, for Barth is to correspond to what has been made possible by Jesus Christ.

I share Herdt's intuition that Barth is one of the great humanists of our time. As I will explain below, my "method" is quite different than Herdt's, yet I think the account I give in *Fully Alive* is compatible with her locating Barth in the Bildung tradition. Barth was a gregarious human being with insight about himself and others. There were some sides to Barth that were less than attractive, but his humanity was undeniable. I hope to show that Barth's theology matched his humanity by helping us see the radical character of a God who would have subjects who enjoy the freedom to glorify God.

Barth's "humanism" is on display in his wonderful book *The Humanity of God*.[3] Barth confessed in that work that his early emphasis on the deity of God, God as "wholly other," threatened to enclose God in a manner that made God's humanity unintelligible. What had to be recognized, Barth argued, is that God's deity includes his humanity, the latter being a Christological claim that is the animating center of Barth's *Dogmatics*. Given Barth's account in *The Humanity of God*, it may seem strange that I have not used his book to develop the theme of this book. Let me explain why.

I want to show that the development of Barth's "humanism" is on full display in his occasional work collected in his book appropriately entitled *Against the Stream: Shorter Post-War Writings, 1946–1952*.[4] I do so under the instruction of Dr. Matt Jantzen, whose dissertation, "Hermeneutics of Providence: Theology, Race, and Divine Action in History," develops Barth's account of providence by directing attention to Barth's reading of the world after the war.[5] Jantzen displays Barth's social and political judgments, what may be called Barth's theological politics, explicitly by showing how the difference that God makes is directly related to what it means to be a human being.

Jantzen's work also makes clear how Barth's understanding of political theology informed why his response to the National Socialists was so different than his response to Russian Communism. I will discuss this at length in the chapters that follow, but Jantzen quite rightly helped me see that Barth saw the National Socialists as having theological significance in a manner that Russian Communism avoided. For Barth, National Socialism was the logical outcome of the European revolution "against Israel and thereby the mystery of the incarnation." A remarkable sentence from a remarkable man.

To suggest that Barth had a political theology is to use a description that was not widely used at the time Barth worked, but in fact to so describe his work is appropriate. The ecclesial and the political for Barth were inseparable.[6] What is required for the recovery of the church for Barth was the disentangling of Christian identity from European identity. According to Barth, for the gospel to be recovered, the reliance the church had formed for centuries with both the pathos and glory of European power must be rejected. Barth's judgments about such matters did not come from nowhere. As his book on nineteenth-century theology reveals, Barth had done his homework in political theory. He saw how liberal theorists' defense of the sovereign state often was a correlate of the judgment that the overriding purpose of life was self-preservation of the individual. According to Barth, as a result the state becomes the agent that enables the individual to pursue their arbitrary desires. The irony, according to Barth, was that a tradition that began as a challenge to the legitimacy of the absolute power of kings ended up legitimating the rule of the bourgeois.

Barth's attacks on the liberal theologians and what he regarded as their high humanism have led many to label him as antihumanistic. Barth, however, never abandoned his presumption that to be a Christian is to be a creature on the way to being a human being. To be sure, that way is one determined by Christ. "God is God and we are not" remains central to Barth, but for Barth the God that is the other is the One that makes us capable of being human.

Barth is the central figure that shapes this book, but I need to be clear. I am in a certain sense using Barth. I am not trying to write about Barth. I have no pretension to be a Barth scholar. Some may even doubt my identification with Barth's project. I think such judgments not entirely fair. The account I give of Barth in *With the Grain of the Universe* I think is "the real Barth." But I am not a Barthian scholastic. I like to think, however, that I work in the spirit of Barth, which is at the same time playful and serious. Barth makes the words of the faith work, and that is a great gift.

In *The Making of Stanley Hauerwas: Bridging Barth and Postliberalism*, David Hunsicker provides an account of Barth's influence on me with which I am in sympathy. Hunsicker argues that, first and foremost,

I share Barth's rejection of Protestant liberalism. I think that is right, though my reasons for the worry about liberalism draw on different philosophical sources than Barth. I am never sure I know what it means to be postliberal, but at the very least it means I have been shaped by the English philosophical tradition that was not on Barth's radar screen.

I am very sympathetic with Hunsicker's account of my relationship to Barth because I find illuminating his somewhat surprising suggestion that our relationship is best understood by attending to Barth's casuistry. Given Barth's criticism of casuistry, that may seem an odd move, but I think it exactly right. It is so because it puts front and center Barth's and my conviction that theology is a descriptive discipline aimed at helping us discover the power of the narrative that is the gospel for determining the way the world is as well as how we are to live in it. Barth, I hope to show, shared my view, "he said with some irony," that theological claims work as a form of practical wisdom.

By focusing on Barth, I hope to counter some of the recent criticism of my work. I am often criticized for overemphasizing the distinctive character of the role of the church; however, more recently I have been criticized for being insufficiently theological. By showing how Barth works to secure theological readings of his time, I hope to show how I have tried to do something similar. To be sure, the way I make theology do work may be odd, but it remains the case that for me, as also for Barth, God matters. In particular I hope to show why it is crucial for theological claims to produce insights that make it possible for our lives to be well lived.

Practical reason feeds on insight. I believe insight is crucial for the work of theology. I suspect I will surprise some because I include chapters on Reinhold Niebuhr not only because Niebuhr was a person of great insight but because Niebuhr and Barth actually encountered one another. I hope to show that, critical of Niebuhr as I am, I continue to read him as an insightful human being. I suspect many find his theology compelling because they think there is a strong correlation between his theology and his insightful declarations. While I would not deny some relation between Niebuhr's theology and his sober assessments of being a human being, I am not convinced his wisdom is grounded in his theology. I think he was first and foremost a person who had little use for false comforts. His honesty prevailed, though that was not sufficient to tempt me to overlook what I can only describe as the thinness of his theology. I hope, however, that the chapters on Niebuhr are sufficient to challenge the presumption that I do not give Niebuhr sufficient credit for his witness. In particular I hope that the chapter on his and Barth's interaction will reflect my admiration for both of these theologians whose shared passion for truth meant they were not about to act as if they agreed.

The chapter on MacIntyre I hope first and foremost will be helpful for those who have not followed his work. MacIntyre is a deep philosopher who is subject to much misunderstanding. I do not expect my chapter will change the minds of those determined to read MacIntyre as a social conservative, but at least I hope my discussion might make those who think it is odd for me to be influenced by Barth and MacIntyre think twice.

The last chapters in this book are responses to specific requests and occasions, but I think the reader will find they display the point about casuistry that Hunsicker develops. The chapter on pastoral theology I think does that as well as anything I have written. If it is the case that "living wisely is most basically a matter of attending to the right words," then I think, as I try to show, Barth was a pastoral theologian.[7] It is unfortunately the case that Tillich became America's theologian for those determined to create a field called pastoral theology.

The chapter on the church in Asia drew me into geographical areas that were unfamiliar. However, I have been made aware that my work is receiving attention in Asia. Again I draw on Barth to suggest how the churches of Asia might find a way to avoid the mistakes of the churches of the West. This requires me to deal with the question of the continuing status of Protestantism. It is often observed that it is unclear in what Christian tradition I stand. This chapter will not satisfy that question, but it may well help explain why I cannot satisfy that question.

The chapter on race revisits the first article I wrote, which was on the Black Power movement. Though I am accused of not sufficiently engaging race and feminist issues, I have written about race more than many think I have. It is certainly the case that I have thought about both in what I hope are constructive ways. I am more sympathetic with the theologies of liberation than many might think. It has been my role to try to help us have a church formed well enough to sustain the struggle against domination. It is my conviction that no theologian is more helpful for that task than Karl Barth. I hope those who are kind enough to read this book will share that judgment. Even more important, I hope they will read more Barth.

I have thought long and hard whether I should include the final chapter, "To Be Befriended," which I wrote before the revelations about Jean Vanier. What we learned about his behavior was a kick in the gut. There is no excuse for what he and his mentor were about. Their spiritual justifications only make matters worse. Yet significant aspects of Vanier's life and thought remain insightful and substantive. This is not the place to explore the complex questions raised by their behavior. All I know to do is mark that this is a subject that will not nor should not go away. I decided to include the chapter to honor Adam.

We live in a time when it is easy to lose track of time. It is important for people to test what day it is—"today is Monday, though we may have lost the significance of 'going to work.'" The pandemic is real and terrible, but Christians are a people not to be determined by despair. It is my hope that in some small way this book may be of help in the project of not losing track of time.

1

The Christian Message in the World Today

Barth Unleashed

Theology is never done in a vacuum. A time and a place are always present in a theologian's work, but that does not mean that the theologian notices or recognizes where they are. Even theologians who try to do theology in a manner that ignores the time and place in which they are working cannot help but reflect a time and place. For example, I sometimes think the assumed apolitical character of systematic theology, that is, theology that seems to give the impression that theology is fundamentally about the relation of ideas, in fact, reflects a politics.[1] In effect, a theology so conceived, particularly after Hegel, often assumes the politics of empire.

Yet it is never easy to know where you are or what time you are in. In particular it is very hard to know where you are theologically. Karl Barth's famous claim that the theologian is to work with the Bible in one hand and newspaper in the other may be good advice, but surely the newspaper is just as likely to mislead as it is to help us know where we are and/or what time we are in. Barth's advocating reading the newspaper fails to answer the question of which newspaper we should be reading. I am not raising the problem of so-called fake news. Rather I am simply calling attention to the different worlds the different headlines of papers presume as well as create.

Barth, however, is a crucial resource for helping us know how to provide an account of where we may be theologically in the world in which we currently find ourselves. I hope to show that Barth was a particularly astute reader of his and, I will suggest, our world. In particular I will direct attention to a collection of Barth's occasional lectures after World War II entitled *Against the Stream: Shorter Post-War Writings, 1946–1952*.[2] I do so because the lectures and essays in that book show that Barth was acutely aware of where he was as well as the implications of that for how he did theology. Barth's judgments about that world are fascinating in themselves, but I am particularly interested in what we can learn from how Barth understood the time and place in which he found himself as a theologian. In the process I hope to suggest how we should understand, to use the title of the journal Barth favored during the war, theological existence today.

The short essays (originally lectures) that make up *Against the Stream* were collected by Ronald Gregor Smith to counter the accusation, an accusation made in a particularly forceful manner by Reinhold Niebuhr, that Barth's work was insufficiently political. Writing as early as 1935, Niebuhr asserted that the "unqualified distinction" between the finite and the infinite in Barth's thought is a heresy from the standpoint of prophetic religion with the result that Barth is unable to make the discriminating political judgments required if Christians are to be responsible social actors.[3] Niebuhr credited Barth for his opposition to the Nazis but thought Barth's refusal to condemn Russian totalitarianism as well as the subjugation of Hungary meant that Barth had no understanding of the principles of justice that represent "the cumulative experience of the race" for dealing with the vexing problems of man's relation to one another.[4]

That Niebuhr could appeal to the "cumulative experience of the race" is a telling indication that he assumed that something like Christendom existed and would continue to exist. Without providing a theoretical account of natural law, Niebuhr seems to have assumed that something like such a law existed. Barth radically calls both assumptions—that is, that we can continue to rely on the resources of Christendom as well as use something like a natural law ethic for social engagements—into question. That he does so I believe to be very important for the future of Christian theology.

Niebuhr was not Barth's only critic. Emil Brunner was perhaps even more concerned about Barth's politics because of Barth's failure to condemn Communism. In "An Open Letter" to Barth from Emil Brunner, a letter included with Barth's response in *Against the Stream*, Brunner challenges Barth to explain why he was so critical of Hitler and Nazi totalitarianism but refused to apply the same criticism to the Russians. Brunner observes that Niebuhr has asked Barth the same question, but they have not received a satisfactory response. Brunner confesses that he and many others find Barth's stance "inexplicable." Even allowing for the different kinds of totalitarianism, it must surely be the case, Brunner argues, that Christians must say an emphatic "No" to all forms of totalitarian politics (106–7).

Barth's answer is illuminative for understanding his way of reading the world as a theologian. He begins his reply by observing that the church must not concern itself with various "isms" and systems but with historical realities as seen in the light of faith and the Word of God. For Barth the church's obligations do not lie in the direction of fulfilling a law of nature but rather toward its living Lord. Therefore, the church never acts on principle but judges spiritually and by individual cases (114). Accordingly, the church rejects every attempt in a Hegelian fashion to systematize political history by refusing to let itself be intimidated by the demand to be up-to-date theologically.

Barth then explains why he reserves judgment about Russian Communist totalitarianism even though it can be as violent as the Nazis. Barth confesses that he did not refrain from declaring Hitler and the Nazis as morally perverse, but he has not condemned the Communist in the same way. He notes that he is well aware of the oppressive character of Russian Communism, but there is a fundamental difference between Russian totalitarianism and the Nazis of Germany. That difference is that the Russians have not attempted to clothe in Christian garments their justifications for the price some must pay in the interest of Communist ideals. According to Barth, the Russian Communists have never committed the basic crime of the Nazis, that is, "the removal and replacement of the real Christ by a national Jesus," nor have they committed the crime of anti-Semitism (140).

Barth's justification for his unqualified condemnation of Nazi Germany and yet his refusal to condemn Russian Communism in similar fashion, I will suggest below, is only intelligible in the light of his theological commitments. Put differently, Barth seems to know how to read where we are because of the kind of God who has made us known in Christ. Such a reading presupposes a narrative about God's care of the world through the cross of Christ. To so read the world, as Barth did, is a crucial skill Barth seems to have developed alongside eating breakfast every morning.

What makes Russian Communism less menacing than the Nazis for Barth is that there is nothing of the false prophet in its makeup. It is not anti-Christian, but it is "coldly non-Christian," which means it is brutally, but honestly, godless (140). By contrast, the challenge the Nazis represented was one that at first seemed to be friendly toward Christianity. Accordingly, the Nazis could use Christian language to cast a spell over the German people so overwhelming that they could no longer distinguish lies from the truth. As a result, the Nazis were able to overwhelm the souls of the Germans by enticing them to call their evil deeds good (115). In short, for Barth the Nazis were particularly perverse because they were a manifestation of "religion."

The persuasive force that empowered the Nazi movement, Barth observes, had a name—Hitler. The challenge Hitler presented for the church was profound just to the extent that Hitler at once seemed to presuppose nihilism yet offered himself as an alternative to nihilism.

For Hitler cast a spell claiming to offer a spiritual alternative in what would otherwise be a world without purpose. Hitler offered a salvation that the church no longer seemed to provide. That is why the Nazis were more dangerous than the Russians.

Barth opposed the Nazis with more vigor than Russian Communism because "it was a matter of life and death, of resistance against a godlessness which was in fact attacking body and soul, and was therefore effectively masked to many thousands of Christian lives" (115). Because Nazism was so spiritually destructive, Barth confessed that he could not forgive the collaborators, particularly those who were cultured, decent, and well-meaning, because of the destructive power of the Nazi ideology. Barth concludes that he considers his intervention into debates in the West about Russian Communism as what was required of himself as a churchman.[5]

I have gone into some detail about Barth's response to Brunner (and Niebuhr) because Barth's reply is as good an introduction as one could desire for Barth's insightful reading of the situation of the church and world after the war. The challenge before the church, according to Barth, was how to read the time and place in the light of Christ. By attending to how Barth reads his world, I hope to illumine the challenges before us given the world we must negotiate as Christians.

Reading Barth's Reading Europe

It was 1946. Barth was giving lectures across war-ravaged Germany. In his dissertation, "Hermeneutics of Providence: Theology, Race, and Divine Action in History," Matthew Jantzen offers an insightful account of Barth's postwar writings to which I am deeply indebted.[6] Jantzen in particular draws attention to Barth's lecture "The Christian Message in Europe Today" as a prime example of Barth's way of reading place and time after the war. Barth, according to Jantzen, argued that the Nazi crisis "revealed a powerful and dangerous theological heresy at the heart of European Christianity as a whole: a distorted conception of divine providence that identifies the content of divine election and incarnation with the person of Western man, thereby sacralizing Western humanity and rejecting the election of the people of Israel and the Incarnation of Christ."[7]

Barth begins "The Christian Message in Europe Today" by observing that Europe has lost its former position as the political, cultural, and religious center of the world. He elaborates on that claim by suggesting that Europe was once the Roman Empire if, as Barth ironically suggests, you remember that not that long ago there was something called the Holy Roman Empire. The legacy of that empire remains enshrined in the European belief that Europe represents the best science, education, religion, and morality that has yet come to realization.

That Europe, the Europe of high humanism, Barth argues has now lost any possibility of claiming to represent the human ideal. That means Barth suggests that Germany can no longer pretend that it is the leading society of Europe and/or that Europe is the leading society of the world. That Europe, the presumptive humane Europe, died in the two world wars. Europe died because those wars so fundamentally called into question the moral and cultural commitments that once made Europe stand for the future of humanity. After those wars, any attempt to recover Europe's past glory as the highest expression of human ideals is now impossible.

What brought about this great change? It was a change that came at the height of European development; it was a change that was at the heart of Europe; it was a change that came as an unparalleled revolutionary movement; it was a change that Barth identifies as a revolution produced by nihilism. Because it was a nihilistic revolution, it could be enacted by mediocre people whose barbarism knew no limit. Barth drives his point home, declaring from "the Christian point of view it was in its most critical aspect, under the name of anti-Semitism, a revolution against Israel and thereby against the mystery of the incarnation of the word of God" (168).

The rise of Hitler, what Barth calls "the great mistake," was not just a German problem but a reality for all of Europe. In particular

Barth calls attention to the 1936 Olympic Games, when the flags of all nations were gathered around the swastika. "The great mistake" began in Germany, but "the bells of the Christian Churches throughout Europe were ringing as though the approaching evil had not already been decided upon definitely, and the death warrant of million upon millions of people signed and sealed" (169), evidence, Barth concludes, that the great German mistake was a European mistake.

Barth asks, what then can be the future? Given the reality that the victory over "the great mistake" was one accomplished not by European forces but by outside forces, it must be the case that the future of Europe is in the hands of non-Europeans. There are only two options—America or Russia. Barth cannot help but think such a choice to be unfortunate. To be sure, America's money and technical skills can be of great use, but Barth wonders if that means Europeans will need to conform to American standards of democracy, ethics, and Christianity. Though he is not in principle anti-American, he worries that Europe's destiny may be to be Americanized (170).

The other alternative of an outside force that has an interest in the remaking of Europe is Russia, which Barth notes is now but another name for Communism. But the rise of Russia also represents the resurgence of the Slavonic races. Russian imperialism is not new but simply the new shape of the imperialism of the czars. That imperialism may awaken the East, raising the question as to whether Europeans have the will or power to protect the remnant of the Western spirit. Europe is destined to be ground between two millstones, which suggests that Europe will be forced to pay for its sins by having its way of life determined by others (171).

Barth thinks there is an alternative. The name of that alternative is "Church." In a letter to the Bernese Pastors' Association, Barth had claimed that "the real Church becomes visible in so far as it emerges and shines forth from its seclusion in ecclesiastical organization, tradition and custom, in the power of the Holy Spirit" (63). Such a church, a church that is visible, can only be seen through faith, but it nonetheless exists. Therefore it is not insignificant that Barth declares that "Christian Churches do still exist in Europe of today" (172). In a devastated Europe the message of the church has been kept alive by the very existence of the church's visibility. That such a church exists means the Christian faith may still determine the life of many in Europe, which can give some basis for a sense of justice and culture being kept alive.

Yet Barth also acknowledges that the Christian churches of Europe have not been able to give the right word at the right time. Pious and clever words are said, but those words have not proved sufficient to put a stop to evil. Accordingly, there has been no sign of a Christian revival in Europe. In the churches and Christian circles there is, among theologians and nontheologians, a stress on restoring rather than reforming the Christian life. As a result, the response of European Christians to the catastrophes that have fallen on them has not proved sufficient to convert those who now identify themselves as non-Christian. Those who hold out some hope that those who recognize that their souls are in danger may think, as the common saying goes, "Necessity leads to prayer," but Barth observes that such a saying cannot be found in the Bible, and even if it were to be found in the Bible, that is not sufficient to make such a saying true (174). Necessity is just as likely to lead to a deadening rather than a conversion of our sensibilities.

Having looked at the Christian message in Europe from the "outside," Barth suddenly shifts gears and says he will now look at the message from the inside, that is, not in the light of history but as it must appear to those who believe the Christian message. The first thing that must be said from such a perspective is that the Christian message can no longer rely upon the fact that it is surrounded and sustained by the glory and pathos of the culture and politics of Europe. The future of the church will have to be enacted in a small and modest sphere: "The Church will have to learn afresh to walk towards its Lord as Peter did, not along smooth paths and up fine staircases with handsome balustrades, but on the water" (175).

The Christian message in Europe must be free and independent. It cannot be dependent on the assumption that it must choose between revolution or tradition, optimism or pessimism, West or East. What the Christian has to say must be said freely, which is only possible if its source is the free grace of God (175). That grace, the free grace of God, is a name, Jesus Christ. In Europe the church's teaching is to proclaim that name: "Jesus Christ is Himself free grace, is himself the Kingdom of God . . . The Europe of today is waiting for Him to be proclaimed anew as the eternal truth bringing freedom to mankind" (177).

That means it is essential that the Christian message not depend on questions of the future of Europe. Accordingly, Barth asks if his readers understand that they can enter the school of the prophets and apostles, which is the most important school there is. Such a school, a school of faith, must train us to be obedient to Jesus Christ. Such obedience and faith are manifest by the "means of our words, our actions, our behavior, our witness, our joy and gratitude, of the origins of our life and of the goal towards which we press" (178).

Jantzen points out that Barth thinks that any attempt to show God's relationship to contemporary political events must begin with the definitive instance of God's presence in history. That presence is of course the incarnation of Jesus Christ. Therefore Barth does not start with some general theory of God's providential relationship to history but with the particular history of Jesus Christ. One must begin with that history because the change enacted in Christ is more determinative than any political change. Put in dramatic but accurate terms, this means that world history is determined by salvation history. Indeed, you only know that a history of the world is possible because of what God has done in Christ.[8]

Barth ends this remarkable lecture with what he characterizes as three questions: The first is the question of love that asks that in obedience to Jesus Christ we not think the worst of every one of those "frightened, miserable, erring, misled, and even godless creatures around us." We must love them for no other reason; if we fail to do so we stand the chance of losing our sense of humor. Second, it must be asked if we are determined to be loyal and faithful to God and therefore to others through right words and actions. And the last question is whether in a world in which it seems that everything that can go wrong has gone wrong, such as the decline of Europe, can the hope necessary to sustain the joy and patience to live positively be possible after such a terrible war (179–80).

Following Barth at a Distance

I assume it is obvious why I think Barth's reflections in *Against the Stream* are so significant. Barth was obviously not an Anabaptist, but his insistence that if the church is to be free, it can no longer depend on the societal and cultural status it enjoyed in the past warms my anti-Constantinian heart. Such a church, moreover, is one capable of being a witness of the free grace of God in Christ. I believe, moreover, that Barth's astute reading of the world after the war has everything to do with that Christological ecclesial stance. Barth could call for the freeing of the church from its European captivity because he saw clearly that the church "cannot allow itself to be hindered by the question of whether and to what extent the European of today, with his particular hopes and fears, will come to meet it, will take an interest in it, favor it and take pleasure in it" (175).

I should like to think that my oft-made claim, a claim I explore at length in the final chapter, that the first task of the church is not to make the world just but to make the world the world, is commensurate with, if not an expression of, Barth's understanding of what it means for the church to be free. Because I have called for the church to first and foremost be the church, I am labeled a sectarian, fideistic tribalist. Barth is usually not so labeled, and I have wondered why, but that is a subject for another time because I am eager to draw on Barth's way of locating his time and place to try to say where we may be.

Much, of course, depends on who the "we" are in the phrase "where we may be." Barth assumed the European "we." That he did so does not seem problematic. He was, after all, Swiss all the way down. That European "we," however, did not stop Barth from writing from the perspective of the Christian "we." The assumption of the Christian "we" by Barth made possible the narrative, a narrative that is present primarily in the background, of Barth's account of Europe.

The Barthian "we," at least the Barthian/German "we," obviously is not the "we" from where I am if I am to try to say where we may be theologically. Just as Barth was by necessity a Swiss/German, so in the same kind of necessity I am Texan/American. To be an American is to be tempted to believe that you represent what everyone would want to be if they had our money and educational opportunity. Thus the presumption is that to be an American is to represent the future because America is the lead society in the world. That is why Americans assume that we represent a universal way of being that is not dependent on a particular time or a place.

The great challenge Christians face in America, particularly given the American presumption that we are a universal people, is how to be God's particular people in a social order determined by universal ideals that once bore the name Europe. The assumption in North American society is that the church is free. Yet the fact that the church is constituted by people who believe that those who actually attend church determine what the church is makes churches so governed anything but free. As a result, the American church is much more secular than the European church because when Americans go to church, they bring their secularity with them. Nothing done at worship challenges the assumption that America is a Christian society and nation. Those who attend church leave church without their identity as Americans ever being challenged. Indeed, the opposite happens because it is assumed that American democracy and American Christianity are the same thing.

The importance of the "we" was brought home to me by Justo Gonzalez's reflections on the claim that we are at the "end of Christendom." He observes that that phrase, when used by Protestant Westerners, usually means, as Barth exemplifies, that Christianity and the church have lost much of the status and influence they once had in the lands of the North Atlantic. From that standpoint the phrase often signals a nostalgic position. Gonzalez, however, observes that when those from the Global South use the phrase, they are thinking of the birth of the "global church that is no longer controlled by the centers of power that held sway long before and long after the 16th century."[9] From such a perspective the phrase "the end of Christendom" indicates hope and celebration.

To make matters even more complex, it is by no means clear whether we are living at the end of Christendom. Barth's general remarks suggested we are. Barth's understanding of the past dependence of European churches on social and cultural expectations as well as state establishments also seems true of North American assumptions, but in some ways the Christendom model is more pervasive in America than in Europe. In an insightful book entitled *Becoming a Christian in Christendom: Radical Discipleship and the Way of the Cross in America's "Christian" Culture*, Jason Mahn argues that those of us who have assumed the passing away of Christendom with the hope that in the process a more vital Christianity will emerge from the ruins have made a fundamental mistake. Mahn challenges the assumption that Christendom is passing away, observing that the ease of becoming a nominal Christian in our society is an indication that a certain form of Christendom is alive and well.[10]

Mahn makes the important point that the claim that secularism has displaced Christendom may be a Trojan horse. What may appear as an act of liberation turns out to reinforce the captivity of the church to America. It does so because our assumption that we can choose to be a Christian turns out to be the means by which the church is held captive. Mahn observes that this may be the most subtle and ironic form of Christendom just to the extent that the church is at the mercy of consumer choice. Capitalism wins again.

Drawing on Douglas John Hall, Mahn identifies another form of Christian imperialism characteristic of more liberal Christians. He notes that mainline churchgoers declared the twentieth century the Christian Century. In various ways they sought to "Christianize" the social order by engendering social support systems through having the state pursue programs that would result in a more relatively just social order. The object was to turn the world into the church, and the effort was largely successful but with the result that the church is left being unintelligible to itself because it can no longer remember why it should exist.[11]

The language employed to try to attract new people to become members of the church is revealing of the continuing form of Christendom Mahn depicts. It is assumed that the vocabulary of the theologies of the past must be translated into more accessible terms in the hope that they can be understood by those who are new to the faith. So translation is required if those who are "unchurched" are to be reached. The description "unchurched" implies that those whom the church is trying to attract are already Christians who just do not know it yet. To confirm their identity as Christians, all they have to do is come to church. Such a strategy assumes that our social order is still suffused with Christian values. As soon as Christians began to use the language of values, you can be sure they no longer believed in God—Nietzsche.

In the next chapter I will say more about the importance of language for the formation of Christians. To be a Christian is to have a vocabulary. Words matter quite literally as matter. They make us who we are. Our lives are less than they should be when we let our language go to seed. There is, moreover, an order to words that makes all the difference. That difference is the difference Christ makes.

The problem of the secularization of the church I think goes deeper just to the extent that the churches that style themselves as evangelical and/or conservative often fail to understand the implications of Barth's Christology. I can illustrate it this way—in a conversation with Swiss Methodists Barth was asked if he thought Methodism showed signs of deviation from the gospel. Barth replied by asking if the Methodists present were aware of the relation between John Wesley and Protestant liberalism. He observed that Methodism, particularly in America, is quite liberal, and that is not an accident because a "great anthropocentric train is at the doorstep of Methodism."

Barth explains what he means by the "great anthropocentric train" by suggesting to the Methodists that they should place the emphasis on Christ and less on the experience of salvation. If they do that, they may avoid the fate of the American church. Barth continues, pointing out that the overemphasis on the salvation experience resembles a person finding themselves on a downhill track not knowing which way the ball will roll. One cannot discuss Christ's resurrection or the virgin birth if the starting point is wrong. The emphasis on experience Barth describes as boggy ground, and Methodism is up to its hips in that mud.[12]

It is not just Methodism that is sunk in the bog; I suspect it as much of the churches that think of themselves as evangelical. People wonder how such people can be on the Religious Right, but Barth's understanding of Methodism makes that politics intelligible. When all you have got is your own experience, you should not be surprised when you end up sleeping with strange bedfellows.

In *Against the Stream* Barth celebrated that the church still existed. The church survived "the great mistake," the terrible destruction of two wars, the decline of Europe, and even persecution. That the church survived, Barth proclaimed, means that the offer which for centuries God has made to humanity through the existence of the church still remains open (172). I wish I had confidence that Barth is right. But I confess I am not sure that the church has survived the world called America. As Mahn argues, it is no easy thing to be a Christian in Christendom. Yet, God is God. Despair is a sin, which means, as we should learn from Barth, that we cannot abandon hope.

We cannot abandon hope. Barth gives us resources, moreover, to help us sustain hope in a hopeless world. Perhaps the most important of those gifts is the gift of language. In the next chapter, therefore, I will explore Barth's ongoing and steady commitment to help us become faithful speakers of the gospel.

2

The Christian Message, the Work of Theology, and the New Humanism

God Matters

"In the shadows of a dying Christendom the challenge is how to recover a strong theological voice without that voice betraying the appropriate fragility of all speech but particularly speech about God."[1] I wrote that sentence to begin a response to the papers by Sam Wells, Jennifer Herdt, and Jonathan Tran that were written for the day set aside to celebrate my retirement from the Divinity School at Duke. I explained that I had only recently found that sentence, but once discovered, the sentence seemed to come as close as I can to expressing the task before us.

To say I found that sentence I know seems odd, given the fact that having just wrote the sentence means I did not find the sentence but rather I just made it up. "Found" implies that the sentence existed before I wrote it, but if I wrote the sentence then I could not have found it. But sentences that matter in a certain sense force themselves on us by expressing what must be said given that what has been said has been said in a manner that makes us say what we did not know we thought. That is a thought that, by the time I finish this chapter, I hope you will not think as confused as you now may think it is. That certain sentences need to be found, moreover, I hope to show is particularly important for the work we do called theology. Barth was to my mind one of the masters of the found sentence.

I call attention to this notion that some sentences are "found" because I think that is particularly true of an aspect of thought, and in particular theological thought, that is seldom noticed. I suspect a theologian's work attracts us, and theology may seldom attract, because of the insights it produces. I suspect, moreover, that most insights feel as if they are "found" rather than the result of some particular effort at thought. That distinction between found and effort may be, however, a false dualism that betrays the insight that insights seem to "jump out at us," having been generated by hard but fruitful thought.

Bernard Lonergan begins his great book *Insight* suggesting that insight is a "supervening act of understanding."[2] He explains that phrase noting that insights seem so simple and obvious that we fail to grasp the conditions that made them possible. In his book of 895 pages he tries to help us gain insight into insight in an effort to help us know what we possess when we possess knowledge. In an admirable summary, however, he declares that insights are apprehensions of contingent relations. That remark may not seem all that significant, but I think it a suggestive way to think about Barth's work.

Barth after all was a theologian of great insight. But he was also a theologian whom many judge to seemingly not attend to the fragility of speech about God or the human. The stark claim that "God is God" and we are not does not have the ring of fragility.[3] The blunt character of Barth's assertion has led many to assume that Barth's theocentric theology implies that the human creature has no role in God's redemption of the world for Barth. Thus it is alleged that Barth provides an inadequate account of what it means to be a human being. He seems to think that to talk of the human means you must speak of God in a very loud voice and of humankind in a whisper.

Barth's lecture, which is included in *Against the Stream,* was given in Geneva in 1949 at a conference that had as its theme "Pour un nouve humanism." The lecture seems to confirm the often-made criticism that Barth's God-centered theology makes God God at the expense of the human. The participants at the conference were philosophers, historians, orientalists, scientists, and Marxists from all over Europe.[4] Barth well knew that most of those at the conference sought a recovery of a humanism that had been lost in the face of the brutality unleashed by two devastating wars. But Barth gave those with such an ambition no quarter. He began his lecture, "The Christian Message and the New Humanism," by pointing out that he and his Roman Catholic colleague at the conference must speak of the actuality of the Christian message, which he acknowledges may be the source of some embarrassment for those gathered at such a conference to celebrate a new humanism.[5]

Barth explains what he means by the "actuality of the Christian message" by suggesting that a theologian at such a conference could not conceal the fact that "with the Christian message it is not a case of a classical humanism nor of a new humanism which is to be rediscovered today, but rather the humanism of God" (184). Jesus is the "actuality of the Christian message" that makes possible our worship of a God who feared not the human.

For Barth the humanism of God names the stark fact that God exists and can be comprehended in a definitive historical form in the life of Jesus Christ. Barth elaborates that claim, observing that "God is not what we think He might or might not be, but God is what he wills Himself to be, in His works and in His revelation of Himself to man" (185).

Barth's declaration that "God is what He wills Himself to be, in His works and in His revelation of Himself to man" is, of course, Barth's way of expressing the implications of his decisive break with Protestant liberalism. Representatives of the liberal theological tradition Barth characterized as only appearing to think about God when in fact they were thinking about man. As he put it, Protestant liberals spoke about God in an exalted tone but "once again and more than ever about this man—his revelations and wonders, his faith and his works. There is no question about it: here man was made great at the cost of God."[6] The reference to "This man" in the preceding sentence is not to Christ but rather is a reference to that character who plays such a strong role in the drama called the Enlightenment, namely, the autonomous individual. That character seeks to be their own creator with the result that they are all the more subject to the tyranny of their own will, which, as it turns out, results in being subject to the arbitrary will of the bureaucratic structures of modernity.

Barth's humanism, therefore, in contrast to the humanism of the Enlightenment, was the humanism of God revealed in the one who is perfectly God and perfectly human, Jesus Christ. In Christ, God and man are one. Barth's robust doctrine of God, rather than distancing him from humanism, in fact meant nothing human was foreign to Barth—after all, he was a person who loved English murder mysteries. For Barth, all things human are to be regarded from the cross of this the Son of God. Such a regard is possible because the dying and later resurrection of Jesus from the grave means no door can prevent him going where he must.

Jesus is no image or symbol of the general reality of the human exactly because he is a singular reality, not an instance of a more universal principle. Again, Jesus is not an "everyman," nor is he some general notion of the human, but he is a Jew born of Mary. Accordingly, Jesus cannot be judged from some general, ostensibly human, point of view, "but rather every human being must be regarded from the point of view of this particular man" (186).

Therefore for Barth the question is not whether God exists. The question is whether we exist. Regarded from a Christian point of view, for Barth that we exist is a miracle of God's love. We did not have to be but we are. That we exist is a manifestation of the kindness of God, who bestows free grace on whom he will: "Man is from God and accordingly belongs wholly to God: purely and simply the object of His creative love and equally a subject devoted to God, His creature, yet a creature possessing free will" (186–87).

Yet we do not exist in the freedom in which we have been created;

we exist in sin. That we do so is a surd for which there is no explanation, but it is a fact that man has strayed from the right way (188). Classical humanism thought it could ignore this judgment about our sinfulness, but Barth observes that after two wars, many of the illusions that were based on this denial of our sins have been taken away. Barth notes, however, that when he reads Heidegger and Sartre, he asks himself whether the spirit of defiance that despises God's free grace remains as sure of itself as it once did (189). Barth's alternative to Heidegger and Sartre is at once an account of our humanity that is nondogmatic and illuminating. In order to show how Barth does what he does, I am going to shift gears by moving in a philosophical direction. I am going to say just a bit about Wittgenstein, at least Wittgenstein read through Toril Moi, because I think his (and her) work help illumine Barth's theocentric humanism. In particular Wittgenstein and Moi help me make clearer that language is at the heart of the matter for helping us understand whose and thus who we are.

Ordinary Language Philosophy

In *With the Grain of the Universe: The Church's Witness and Natural Theology*, I began the penultimate chapter, which was entitled "The Witness of Barth's *Church Dogmatics*," with Barth's statement, or better, his confession, "We can only repeat ourselves."[7] I suggested that Barth's observation that he could only repeat himself reflected his discovery that the God who has found us in Christ makes possible the finding of ourselves within the confusions we call our life. Such a finding is only available through mediation, which requires, just as a musical score may require, repetition if we are to understand its truthful goodness and beauty. Thus Barth's style of writing theology in the *Dogmatics* is commensurate with its content. Barth could only repeat himself, and in effect the *Church Dogmatics* in volume after volume is one long repetition, because he only has one thing to say. What he has to say is, Jesus is Lord.

In a sense, that Barth could only repeat himself makes the *Dogmatics* closer to poetry than to what might be considered more systematic philosophical or theological work. Like the poet, Barth works to make language do work that helps us understand how you cannot distinguish what the poem is about from the language used. In that sense, Barth's performance is not unlike Wittgenstein's remarks just to the extent Wittgenstein takes you through one exercise after another in the hope you will "get it." Barth and Wittgenstein write in a manner that will not let us forget we are human.

In her recent book *Revolution of the Ordinary: Literary Studies after Wittgenstein, Austin, and Cavell,* Toril Moi has an account of Wittgenstein and the philosophy of language that is instructive for helping me say what I have just been trying to say. As far as I know, Moi has no theological interests. Her book is an extended introduction to ordinary language philosophy and in particular the work of Stanley Cavell. Though she is a literary scholar like many people in the fields generally known as the humanities, she is determinatively interdisciplinary, or, perhaps more accurately, nondisciplinary.

She begins her book by declaring that her principal thesis or purpose in writing the book is to show that "ordinary language philosophy has the power to transform prevailing understanding of language, theory, and reading in literary studies today."[8] That transformation, according to Moi, means that though she is identified as a literary scholar, she has little stake in maintaining a concept like "literature" in order to legitimate or at least sustain the academic discipline called literary studies. But she also thinks the skills acquired through the exercises entailed by ordinary language philosophy can help develop the attention to language that can make us better readers of the texts scholars in literature identify as crucial for determining "the field." I obviously think that is also true for readers and writers of theology.

Moi observes that one of the problems of trying to show what we can learn from ordinary language philosophy is the very description "ordinary language philosophy." That description unfortunately invites misunderstanding of what is meant by the phrase "ordinary language." As a result, some associate ordinary language philosophy with the development of positivistic forms of analytic philosophy that began at Oxford after World War II. That mode of analytic philosophy led to the general assumption by many that "ordinary" meant that the subject of ordinary language philosophy was unreflective conventional common sense. Moi, drawing on the work of Richard Fleming, protests that to so understand ordinary language philosophy is a profound mistake. Deeply informed by Wittgenstein and Cavell, Moi argues that ordinary language philosophy is best understood as the attempt to draw attention to the exemplary, public, and shared "necessary order of our common existence" (8). "Necessary order of our common existence" is a loaded phrase that I will say more about by way of Moi's account of Wittgenstein.

In the *Philosophical Investigations,* Wittgenstein says one of his tasks is to "bring words back from their metaphysical to their everyday use." Moi observes that he does that by assembling reminders of what we already know, that is, how we are at home in our use of words. That means we have no need to try to improve ordinary language because the distinctions we need to express ourselves as human beings we already have at hand (74). Just think what it would feel like if we did not have locutions such as, "As I meant to say" or "I am sorry." It is important to note that Wittgenstein is not saying that everything we say is unproblematic. Rather he is simply calling attention to the fact that we seldom notice that our language works because of the work it is in fact doing.

"Ordinary language," therefore, is not the name of a particular kind of language, it is not a name for something called "everyday" expressions, it is not the language of "the common man," nor is it some standard language. Rather, ordinary language is "what we say" when what we say does work. It is ordinary language that "helps us draw distinctions, carry out tasks, engage fruitfully with others—in short, language as the medium in which we live our lives" (181).

Yet some worry that without a full-blown metaphysical account of language we cannot avoid some form of skepticism. The focus on ordinary language does not promise that skepticism can be defeated in principle, but it turns out that the attempt to defeat skepticism in principle is one of the generative sources that produced skepticism. Thus the widespread assumption that if we are to avoid skepticism, words must in some way hook onto reality to reflect the way things are. Words, it is thought, must represent some object to have a meaning that is not arbitrary. Such a view is widely assumed by many to be necessary in order for a language to reflect the way things are.

In order to get such a view on the table, Wittgenstein begins the *Investigations* by quoting a passage from Augustine in which Augustine reports that as a child he learned how to speak by observing how words gained their meaning by having and/or referring to a corresponding object. If that were not the case, Augustine seemed to suggest, words would have no meaning. Though Wittgenstein was a great admirer of Augustine, he thought Augustine had made a fundamental mistake by thinking that the meaning of a word is its reference. He thought that must be an important mistake because, as he observed, any mistake by Augustine must be important for someone with such a powerful mind to make it. Accordingly, Wittgenstein took as one of his tasks to free us from Augustine's picture of how language works, that is, from the mistaken view that we learn the meaning of a word by pointing to a referent.[9]

The way Wittgenstein goes about that task is by providing examples for thought. They can be thought of as exercises meant to establish new or reinforce old habits. But, as Moi observes, that makes it very difficult to write about Wittgenstein's philosophy because Wittgenstein does not have a position; at most he has a task. He sought to do nothing less than to help us recover the significance of what we say by freeing our words from philosophical and metaphysical theories to return them to their everyday use because that is where they do their work. So Wittgenstein is not a philosopher with a position, but, more interestingly Wittgenstein sets out to help us say why we say the things we do.

The temptation is to attribute to him some doctrine—"meaning is use"—which certainly has a place in his thought. But "meaning is use" is not an alternative theory to Augustine that works to explain how words gain their meaning, that is, you know the meaning of a word by its use. Wittgenstein carefully says in the *Investigations* (43) that "for a large class of cases—though not for all—in which we employ the word 'meaning' it can be defined thus: the meaning of a word is its use in the language."[10] It is extremely important to note that Wittgenstein says "for a large class of cases" as well as his conditional, "in which we employ the word meaning." Those two clauses make clear that "meaning is use" is not a general theory.

Moi rightly puts the matter this way: "Wittgenstein gives us no theory that can be summarized and used, but rather gives us a radical alternative to theory. He teaches us to give up theory's craving for generality and instead look to examples" (1). Examples turn out to be the heart of the matter because they teach us how we use words. Or, in one of Wittgenstein's often-repeated phrases, he suggests that examples "teach us how to go on." Learning how to go on by attending to examples helps us to discover that we learn language and the world together (77).

Yet it is nonetheless true, as Moi contends, that the heart of Wittgenstein's criticism of Augustine begs for elaboration. Wittgenstein's problem with Augustine's picture of how language works is primarily directed at Augustine's concentration on representation. The idea presumed by Augustine was that the essence of language is to be found in the necessity of every word gaining its meaning by the object it represents. Such a view is wrong. It is wrong first and foremost because language does not have an essence (26). According to Moi, Wittgenstein is trying to help us see that language is doing too many things to be limited to a representational function. That means that the choice between realism and idealism is a false choice once it is recognized that for most of what we say there is no gap between a word, its meaning, and the world (13).

It is certainly true, however, that Wittgenstein thinks the meaning of a word often is to be found in its use. For Wittgenstein words do things. Moi quite rightly warns against turning "meaning is use" into a general theory because use is not a general explanation; rather, the use of an expression "is a practice grounded on nothing. Use is simply what we do. Nothing—no essences, no built-in referential power—obliges us to continue using language as we do now. In fact, we don't always continue: language is a constantly changing practice" (29). It is important to note that Wittgenstein is not denying that representation is one of the things we do with language. What he denies is that there is only one thing language does; therefore no single theory can adequately capture all the work language does for us.

The temptation is to assume that when asked, "What does a word mean?," we think we need to supply an explanation or definition to nail down the meaning of the word. Explanations are meant to respond to specific problems such as those created when someone wants to know how words like "red" or "apple" have any meaning. But that picture is deeply misleading because we do not teach a child to speak by explaining how words are used. Rather children and others who do not know the language are trained to know how to use the word. Moi quite rightly suggests that the distinction between training and explanation is crucial because training requires constant practice, whereas explanation entails the giving of reasons, which must at some point come to an end. Training is the key that makes the Augustine quotation all the more interesting, centering as it does on the role training plays for our ability to understand one another. If I am asked, for example, how I know there are five apples in a basket, I can only reply, "I speak English."

In *The Claim of Reason: Wittgenstein, Skepticism, Morality, and Tragedy*, Stanley Cavell provides a lovely example of how training works by telling us about how his very young daughter learned from her baby book the word "kitty." She made the sound "kitty" and pointed to the kitty in her book. Some weeks later, however, she stroked a fur piece and said "kitty," making Cavell realize that she really does not know what kitty means. Cavell suggests it is only when she gets to stroke a litter of kittens that she will "walk into speech."[11]

Moi observes that for Wittgenstein words and practices are intertwined. To find out what a word means is to learn something about the world. To learn something about the world "is learning to see. Learning to see is learning the world" (33). To learn a language is, therefore, to acquire a world. When the practices that give rise to a language die, the language will die. The language may not die when the practice dies, but it will more likely become a language on a holiday. That means the language no longer is doing or can do any work.

Moi suggests that the alternative to how our language can go on holiday is to attend to what Wittgenstein meant by a form of life. Forms of life are conventions that constitute and give shape to our lives. Forms of life can vary from mailing a letter to signing a marriage contract. Forms of life, however, reflect our bodily form as well as learned behaviors. For example, Cavell notes that for Wittgenstein learning a language means we learn not only what the names of things are but what the name is. For example, we learn not merely the form of expression for expressing a wish, but we learn what or how a wish is expressed. To learn a language, therefore, is to learn to know a phenomenon such as heat, although most of us will not know heat the way a physicist knows heat. In the same way, the love of a child can develop in distinctive ways. Moi climaxes her account of form of life by calling attention to Cavell's suggestion that if one grows up to become a Christian theologian, they will possibly learn even more (56).

From Moi's perspective, however, theology is one thing and literature quite something else. Moi has little use for all attempts at trying to define literature in order to justify the institutionalization of a field in a university's curriculum. The very attempt to group certain literatures together by providing a definition of "literature" that can determine who is in and who is out, Moi argues, is not only a mistake but suggests a deeply misleading view of what the study of literature does.

Drawing on Cavell's account of acknowledgment as a response to the expressions of another, Moi argues that literature is training in the practice of acknowledgment. We must be trained to understand the judgments of others, which means we must attend to the reasons and motivations for people saying and doing what they say and do. Accordingly, literary criticism cannot be done without also revealing our own judgments (217). This, moreover, Moi observes, is not as straightforward or easy as it seems. Training is required.

One of the essential forms of that training is learning to read. Moi again refers to Cavell's understanding of reading as a form of acknowledgment. Acknowledgment is a central theme in Cavell. It is so because Cavell understands acknowledgment to be the form our lives must take in recognition of our finite character. Acknowledgment is a response that suggests I must do something given what I know (107). Skepticism is often the appropriate response to our inability to know another human being—thus the role of Shakespeare's *King Lear* in Cavell's work. Moi observes we assume a novel or play is harder to read than a theory or philosophy, but she argues that is a mistake because she suspects we think the novel is harder only because we lack the practice of reading novels.

To learn to be a reader is to learn how to be a human being. Reading is the practice that educates our experiences. We lack the power to understand our own experience, but our experience can be trained by art and the everyday. Such a training I think is what we gain by learning to read Karl Barth.

The Language of Theology

I am fairly confident that Barth never read or studied Wittgenstein, but I hope to suggest that the way he did theology is illumed by the affinities Barth has with Moi's account of Wittgenstein's and Cavell's work. In particular Barth left behind both conservative and liberal forms of theology that produced and reproduced the assumption that theological language had to be made meaningful by supplying a theory of reference. Barth offers no theory of how we can talk of God or the human—he can only repeat himself, but in the repetition we discover what and how the knowledge of God makes possible knowledge of what being a human being entails.

Barth offers no theory to secure the meaningfulness of theological speech, but the whole of the *Dogmatics* can be read as an alternative to theory. The *Dogmatics* is a training manual that teaches us how to talk. Barth's reflections on the Jesus parables make this explicit. He observes that the New Testament parables were the prototypes of the order in which "there can be other true words alongside the one Word of God, created and determined by it, exactly corresponding to it, and fully serving it and therefore enjoying its power and authority."[12]

In an extraordinary article, Jonathan Tran suggests that by attending to ordinary language philosophy we can show how theological language works by attending to what can and cannot be said.[13] Wittgenstein explored what can and cannot be said by making compelling remarks that force further thought. I want to suggest that though Barth used more words than Wittgenstein, there is an interesting relation between the way Barth did theology and Wittgenstein's philosophy. Neither Wittgenstein nor Barth had a theory that limited what could or could not be said. Rather, what both supplied was one example after another to train us to recognize ourselves by what we can and cannot say.

For example, Barth begins the foreword to the English edition of his great book *Dogmatics in Outline* with the observation that these lectures, which were delivered in the ruins of the University of Bonn not long after the end of World War II, were called systematic theology. But as I noted in the first chapter, Barth observes that "systematic theology" is a term that is as paradoxical as a "wooden iron." Barth confesses that unlike Tillich, he could never write a book under the title "Systematic Theology." He could not use that title because "system" suggests thought constructed in terms of fundamental conceptions in accordance with a certain philosophy that is determined by a method. Barth notes that theology cannot be subject to such a method because the subject of Christian theology is to be found in history, which means the God that is the subject of theology is free.[14]

In *Dogmatics in Outline,* Barth's extraordinary commentary on the Apostles' Creed, he lays out his understanding of the language of theology. He begins by making clear that the first responsibility of the church is to trust in God's word and the knowledge that in Jesus Christ the church has been given the truth, which the church must confess. Accordingly, there is no reason to try to get behind the language we have been given once it is recognized that God's people possess and are thereby possessed by their own language. That language has been shaped by the special history of its life with God. It is the language of faith, which is the same language of public responsibility, in which Christians must speak. When the church does not confess in its own language, it does not confess at all.[15]

The church's proclamation is language. It is not an accidental, arbitrary, chaotic, and incomprehensible language. It is a language that comes forward with the claim to be true. It upholds itself as the truth against the lie. The confession Christians make, therefore, is not irrational, but the form rationality takes when what is confessed we believe is true.[16] For example, consider Barth's reflection on the word "God," a set of reflections I suspect Wittgenstein would have loved.

Barth observes that the word "God" seems to refer to a reality that is familiar to the history of religion and philosophy. Thus when people speak of God, Barth notes they think they are speaking of a being that is universally present, and/or the object of human homesickness or the human hope for a unity, and/or the basis for existence having some meaning, and/or a Supreme Being that determines all that exists. Each of these ways of speaking of God reflects deeply human desires that there be such a god or gods. But Barth then thunders that the Christian God is not to be confused with any god so understood. The Christian God is not to be found in such a series of gods or in a general concept of the divine. The God of the Christian confession is not the fulfillment of human desires but the One who exists in a completely different way than those called divine. One could not hope to have a clearer account of the difference the concrete character of language should work.[17]

That does not mean, however, that Christian language can only be used or heard in the church. The church exists for the sake of the world. Where confession is serious and clear, the speech of the church must be able to illumine our everyday speech. The kind of speech, for example, that can be found in the newspaper. Barth maintains such speech is necessary if Christians are to speak straightforwardly about the complicity of Christians with the rise of Hitler and the German Christians. The church at that time did not say the "No" that her language and faith demanded. Yet one thing is clear: when the church does not confess in its own language, it usually fails to confess at all.[18]

The language of the church is the language of a people who are in an ongoing endeavor to be witnesses to the truth of Jesus Christ. That truth is not one truth among others, but it is *the* truth that creates all truth. If a person believes that life has meaning and, therefore, there is a way to rightly live, there is no context in which it is intelligible for them to ask if their life has purpose. They exist to glorify God through the words we have been given.

The very character of the *Dogmatics* reflects Barth's understanding of how we must be trained if we are to talk right as Christians. Thus the repetitive character of the *Dogmatics* suggests that Barth understood he was preparing a training exercise for Christians who no longer had available past exercises. Wittgenstein gives you one thought experiment after another. Barth gives you another volume to help Christians recover how to talk. There is no shortcut, moreover, for learning how to talk right. It may not take fourteen volumes, but it cannot hurt to have all fourteen.

You may be wondering what all this has to do with Barth's understanding of the new humanism. I think it helps us understand better Barth's humanity and how that humanity informed his theology. In the first chapter I observed that there was no freestanding anthropology in Barth. What it means to be a human being cannot be answered separate from the God who became one of us. As I suggested above, that strong theocentric position Barth understands to underwrite an equally robust humanism. Some find that his humanism is more an expression of Barth the human being rather than Barth the theologian. But if I am right, there is no Barth the human being who is not Barth the theologian. And that Barth was determined to train us to be a human being who found their humanity in the worship of the One of us who was and remains without sin.

"In the shadows of a dying Christendom the challenge is how to recover a strong theological voice without that voice betraying the appropriate fragility of all speech but particularly speech about God." That is the sentence with which I began this chapter. In the first chapter I said a bit about what I take to be a "dying Christendom," but I do not pretend to have treated that subject adequately. At the very least, perhaps that dying will make possible the recovery of our language that we might again be for the world what God would have us to be, that is, those who know how to pray with words.

3

The Church and Civil Society

Political Theology

"The first task of the church is not to make the world more just but to make the world the world." I called attention to that sentence in the first chapter. I did so then and do so now because that sentence has earned me the label of being a sectarian, fideistic tribalist. Those labels are meant to convict me of a betrayal. I am allegedly trying to convince Christians that we must withdraw into ecclesial enclaves rather than attempt to create more nearly just societies. I am more or less accused of being an ecclesial fundamentalist who thinks the church is more important than God. In effect, it is thought I am trying to reverse the insights of the social gospel as well as the realist expression of the social gospel associated with Reinhold Niebuhr.[1] Even more outrageous, it seems I do not appropriately appreciate the significance of liberal democracies and why Christians have a stake in societies and states in which democracy flourishes.

Before you get too nervous, I have good news for you: I have no intention of going over the well-plowed ground in which I defend myself from the above accusations. I have said all I am going to say in response to those charges. I think it serves no one well for me to say, "No, I am not," with the expected response, "Yes, you are." "No, I am not" and "Yes, you are" may make a good popular-song lyric, but it gets us nowhere for helping find our way as Christians in the world in which we now find ourselves.

Though I am not going to try to convince you that I am not a sectarian, I am going to use this chapter to locate how I ended up with the opening sentence. People assume that I came to believe that the church must be first and foremost the expression of the politics of the gospel under the influence of John Howard Yoder. I certainly have been influenced by Yoder, but before Yoder it was Barth who put me on the path that has led me to try to recover the political character of the church. "The political character of the church," however, is a phrase begging for clarification. I am going to try to clarify that phrase by providing an account of Barth's theological politics.

I will again direct attention to *Against the Stream* and, in particular, Barth's important essay "The Christian Community and the Civil Community."[2] It is important to note, however, that this essay was also included in a book that collected several of Barth's occasional essays about politics entitled *Community, State, and Church*.[3] I call attention to this book because even though Will Herberg wrote an appreciative account of Barth's political theology, he concluded his introduction with a Niebuhrian critique of Barth's refusal to condemn Communism with the same intensity he had condemned Nazism. As a result of that book, Barth was characterized as being "politically naïve." As I will try to show, the essays in that book itself show Barth as anything but naïve. Barth was, to be sure, misunderstood exactly because the way he thought about political theology did not fit into the current conceptual schemes.

It has become increasingly clear that Barth's theology and his politics are so intimately interrelated that there is no way to say where one begins and the other stops. In an early essay on the controversies in Europe occasioned by Marquardt's contention that Barth's theology is driven by his socialist convictions, George Hunsinger rightly argued that, for Barth, theology and politics each has its own integrity, which requires that theology must not be politicized nor politics theologized. Rather, what must be acknowledged is that for Barth theology will make its contribution to politics only by remaining theology and vice versa.[4] Yet Barth at an event at Union Seminary in New York admonished those gathered to hear him that if they were to say anything about him, they should not "forget to say that I have always been interested in politics."[5]

That is probably to put the matter in language that betrays Barth's passion for politics. He was not just "interested" in politics, but the very way he did theology was meant to be a politics.[6] By directing attention to Barth's chapter in *Against the Stream,* I hope to show how Barth's development of the analogies between theological claims and forms of political organization were not, as often was alleged, arbitrary.[7] By attending to Barth's "method," I hope to make clear why my call for the church to be the church is not a retreat from the "politics of Jesus."

Before I discuss in detail Barth's political theology, however, I need to say more than I have in the first two chapters about Barth's understanding of what had happened to the church as the result of two world wars. As I suggested above, Barth thought it was clear that Christendom was coming to or had come to an end. In the essay "The Christian Community in the Midst of Political Change," he observes that recent events have made apparent how "the morality of modern civilized man has turned out to be a terribly thin covering over a sea of primitive barbarity" (57). Artists pledged to help us acknowledge who we have become can offer nothing more than confirmation of our own disintegration. The churches have seldom given a clear witness about this disaster, but it all adds up to the necessity of recognizing that "the whole conception of a Christian civilization in the West has been pitilessly exposed as an illusion" (57).

Barth then addresses the young who must inherit such a world. If they are to exercise their freedom, they must accept the responsibility that goes with such freedom. The temptation of the young will be, Barth suggests, to overindulge in technics, sport, and aesthetic amusements, which cannot help but produce a kind of mindlessness which makes people prey to the slogans of charlatans and dictators. As a result, the young will be tempted to find refuge in skepticism or intellectual nihilism. So Barth sees the challenge before the church: if it is to be an alternative to such a world, it must reclaim its visibility (60–62).

Barth, therefore, assumed that the challenge before war-devastated Europe was a matter of how to foster hope in hopeless world. I do not think I need to spend space suggesting how the very brief account I have just given of Barth's understanding of the European world after 1945 has remarkable similarity to our world. That similarity may, however, be the reason I so identify with Barth's call for a recovery of the visible church. A call for the church to recover its visibility I think is necessary if the church is to reclaim its political character.[8] Barth rightly emphasizes that Christians can only see the "real church" through the eyes of faith because the visibility of the church is only made possible by the work of the Holy Spirit. Such a church, a church that is gathered, is one whose faithfulness to Jesus means it is held and sustained over an abyss, but by it being so positioned, those called to it discover they are in absolute solidarity with one another (64–69).

Barth's most fundamental ecclesial convictions seem to be of the free church variety. In answer to a question from a Swiss Methodist in 1961 concerning whether Barth judged the state church or the free most faithful to the New Testament, Barth acknowledged he inclined toward the free church because the state church is always "something bad." But Barth went on to explain that it does not matter whether you belong to a state church or free church because a state church can be a confessing church, the description Barth prefers to state or free church, and a free church may equally fail to be a faithful church. For Barth, that is a reminder that what makes a confessing church—a faithful church—is action. To be sure, the actions required for the church to be the church are those actions prompted by the Holy Spirit. That is not a surprise, but what is a surprise is how Barth understands the theological status of the state.

Before developing Barth's understanding of "the state," I need to call attention to a problem in Barth's discussion of "the state" that Barth does not address directly but is a major challenge for his enterprise. His use of the phrase "the state" is an abstraction that dulls the Christian imagination about God's care of the neighbor through the work of "governing authorities." As my friend David Aers, a scholar of the late Middle Ages, reminded me, most people in most of human history did not live in what we assume is "the state." Pontius Pilate was not a state functionary. He was a functionary in a complex and massive empire—an empire may have a state but not necessarily. "The state" can relieve Christians of the necessity to grapple with the messy and confusing character of history. Barth wanted to avoid all abstractions and attend to the historical moment, but, as we shall see, that proves to be more difficult than he thought.

Barth on the State

In a discussion in Budapest in 1948, Barth was asked if the state belongs to the sphere of creation or the sphere of redemption. His reply is illuminating: "The State belongs to the order of redemption. It is no accident that the place where the State appears in the Creed is in the second article ('suffered under Pontius Pilate') and not in the first article." Barth develops this claim by suggesting that the state is an institution of God's wisdom and patience, which means God's work cannot be divided into various departments. The state embodies God's intention to see that His mercy has scope on the earth, which is the purpose of creation itself.

In the essay in *Community, State, and Church* entitled "Church and State," Barth explicitly connects this understanding of the state as redeemed with Romans 13. In particular he argues that the God who so orders the work of the state in Romans 13 cannot be understood apart from the person and work of Christ. It is crucial, therefore, that God not be understood in some general way as Creator and/or Ruler as the Reformers did. Rather, when the New Testament speaks of the state, Barth maintains, "we are, fundamentally, in the *Christological* sphere."[9] Accordingly all attempts to provide an explanation of the origin of the state as something fated, historically necessary, or established by contract cannot be sufficient. The state is one of God's creatures.

That the state exists as a redeemed creature means that even if a state betrays its divine calling, it cannot escape God's purpose for the founding of the state. Barth explains that the state is an attempt by men to organize their outward life. The order created is order maintained by force. But no force is finally adequate to guarantee order, which means the state must be supported by the "free responsibility of its members." The state cannot enact the salvation found only through the church, but it remains true that we need the state no less we need the church (95).

States do go wrong, but that is not sufficient reason for Christians to withdraw from their commitment to seek justice. For example, a state that would go so far as to honor evildoers does not mean that the Christian attitude toward the state should change. The Christian must have faith that God will find ways to call into existence those who would keep the state true to its task of maintaining the freedom of the church. By doing so, the state depends on Christians who recognize that even if the state betrays its primary task, which is to ensure free preaching of the gospel, it "will nevertheless be constrained to fulfill its function" through the suffering of the followers of Christ.[10] It is important to remember that Barth could oppose the Nazis exactly because they would not allow the free preaching of the gospel.

Barth maintains that there is a close relation between the existence of the state and the church, but that does not mean the church cannot seek to become the state or the state seek to become the church. They differ because the church is gathered through free individual decisions, whereas the state is constituted by those living within its boundaries.

The state, therefore, is necessarily coercive because those who come under its authority did not do so as a calling. They may think they have chosen to be under this or that state's control, but that is self-deception.

That the state has that character is why, as Romans 13 suggests, the state does not wield the sword in vain. The state is constituted by law, which can only be established and maintained through force.[11] There is a law internal to the life of the church, but the church is not a juridical entity like the state because the church does not employ methods of compulsion to compel obedience as well as punish those who do not obey. When the church mimics the coercive methods of the state, when the church becomes a Constantinian church, it proves to be its undoing.

The church, however, has no theory of the state in the sense that the church knows what the state ought to look like. The church must avoid abstract norms, ideals, and sociopolitical ideologies. Of course the church will be interested in political changes, but the "church must be and must remain a Christian fellowship and live for its own concerns even in the midst of political changes" (78). Christians who must not resist political changes must judge any developments in light of the decisive change enacted in the life and death of Jesus Christ. This is the news that the world must hear. Such a hearing will be difficult if Christians are busy trying to create Christian parties or Christian states. The Christian's first duty is to always obey God rather than men, but being so established, the next most important thing for the Christian to do for the state is not lose their calm or sense of humor (98).

Yet Barth does maintain that the church must not concern itself with various political "isms" and/or systems, but rather with historical realities seen in the light of faith. In particular the church should never act on a presumed law of nature. There may be a "natural law" that embodies what is regarded as universally right or wrong, but for the church to adopt natural law as the basis of its political engagement means the church can never be sure it is not acting on an illusion (28). The church, therefore, never thinks, speaks, or acts "on principle" but rather judges spiritually individual cases. Yet there is a method to such judgments that would make no sense if Barth did not view the state Christologically. I will now try to show how that works.

Barth's Analogies

The report I have just given about Barth's non-Constantinian stance toward the state might give the impression that Barth thought that, when it comes to the state, we lived in a night in which all cows are gray. That, however, is not the case. He developed what I can only think to describe as exercises of thought that are meant to help Christians use what they have learned from the politics of the church to imagine what kind of political alternative they should work for the politics outside the church. This "method," and I am not sure it can be called anything so grand as a "method," is possible because of Barth's insistence that the state has been redeemed. Barth stresses that does not mean the state has an autonomy or independence over against the church, nor can church and state be equated. But the possibility remains to regard the existence of the state as an allegory, as a correspondence and an analogue to the Kingdom of God which the church preaches and believes in (32).

As a civil community, the state cannot know the mystery of the Kingdom of God, and, therefore, it cannot know what creates the possibility of its own existence. The state, accordingly, can only draw from "the porous wells of the so-called natural law," but it cannot without the church move toward the righteousness that is the Kingdom of God. The state "needs the wholesomely disturbing presence, the activity that revolves directly around the common center, the participation of the Christian community in the execution of political responsibility" (33). So what is obligatory for the church is a possibility for the state. Accordingly, Barth thinks he has established the grounds for exploring analogies between the church and the state that are meant to help Christians discern how the state should and can be ordered and served in the world in which we find ourselves.

It is not necessary to give a detailed account of these analogies, but

I need to say enough to show how they work to provide examples to produce thought.[12] I will not discuss them in the same order Barth does because I do not think he thought the order to be of particular significance. For my purposes it is more important to get a sense of the whole. Barth begins his examination of the analogies, as one would expect, with Christology. Thus his claim that if the eternal God became a man, which he surely did, it is imperative that the church in all times and places be first and foremost concerned about each particular human being. The most wretched of people must be defended against all who would subordinate their humanity to a cause. For Barth there is simply no place for a utilitarian calculus in which one person can be used for the good of another and/or even the good of the whole society. It is the role of law to protect us from the temptation to use a person for some abstract good. That is why it is so important that the state be based on the order the law provides. Just as Christ came to save the lost, so the church must insist that the lowest in society be protected by the law.

Because the church is a witness of the act in which God in Jesus Christ established the original claim on men and women, the church will be found where all political activity is disciplined by the law. That is why the church always stands for a constitutional state and against tyranny or anarchy. Because the church is a witness that the Son of Man came to seek the lost, the church must always be first concerned with the poor as well as those who are socially and economically weak. The church must stand for justice in the political sphere, which means supporting those policies that are more likely to help those who are the most vulnerable.

The church is the fellowship of those called by the love of God to be the children of God, which means that the church must work to protect the basic right of every citizen to be free. Such an understanding of freedom, however, is at odds with the assumption that the state must allow the citizen to do whatever they desire. Rather, the freedom that is to be sustained is that necessary for citizens to act responsibly for the good of their neighbor. Accordingly, the family, education, art, science, religion, and culture are to be safeguarded from state control.

The church is the fellowship of those who are members of the one Body whose Head is Christ. As one so constituted, they are bound and committed to securing for each the freedom of the whole. Accordingly, the church's approach to collective responsibilities is neither individualistic nor collectivistic but rather a ministry of the congregation. As a community that lives on the basis of baptism in the one Spirit, the church must stand for the conditions that ensure the freedom of adult citizens that is necessary for the meeting of their responsibilities. That means that restrictions on certain classes, races, and sexes are arbitrary conventions and can no longer be justified.

The church is a community of a variety of gifts, which means in the political sphere that there is the need to separate different functions and powers such as the legislative, executive, and the judicial. Correlatively that means no human being should occupy the functions of legislation and ruler in the name of serving the people. In a similar fashion, because the church lives in the light cast by the day of the Lord, the church must be the sworn enemy of secret policies and diplomacy. Statecraft that is anarchic and/or tyrannical flourishes on keeping itself hidden, which means the church has the duty to expose states so constituted. Such a duty expresses the fundamental stance of Christians, which is one of service rather than ruling. Internal to the church, there are forms of rule that are also forms of service, but that is not the case in the politics of the state. As an aside, Barth observes that Hitler's rule was based on sheer naked power, which is diseased.

The church is ecumenical and catholic by its very origin, which means it resists all abstract local and national interests in the political sphere. The key word is "abstract" because Barth argues that the church will always seek to serve the concrete place in which it finds itself. Yet, because each church is tied to other local churches, it must also look beyond the walls of the city. It nevertheless is the case that the church will always seek first to serve the welfare of the place it is stationed.

Finally, the church knows God's anger and judgment but also knows that God's anger lasts only for a moment, whereas His mercy is for eternity. The political analogy of this is that the violent solutions for the conflicts in political communities from police measures to armed risings against regimes to defensive wars waged by lawful states must be approved, supported, and, if necessary, even suggested by the Christian community. But Barth adds that the church may show its inventiveness by searching for other solutions before the necessity of violence.

Barth concludes these analogies by suggesting that they are anything but a full political theory; at most they are a few examples of Christian choices and activities in the political sphere. They are not equivalent to paragraphs in a constitution of a state, but rather they are illustrations for how Christians can make political decisions that are based in their theological convictions. He explains that he used examples because he was trying to illuminate the relationship to the gospel and certain political decisions and modes of behavior. Yet he notes that as transitions from one sphere to another, they will never be open to absolute proof because they will always need to be particularized (42).

If it is objected that Barth's analogical method is a rather artificial way to say Christians should support democratic regimes, Barth, I suspect, would receive such an objection with a good deal of humor. In fact, he is quite candid that the "Christian line" he developed as based on the gospel has a striking tendency to support the side of what is generally called the "democratic state." He acknowledges he has no desire to deny the obvious. But he warns that democracies are just as likely as autocratic states to be subject to anarchy and tyranny. If democracy means the will of the people, it remains powerless to describe the kind of state that corresponds to the divine ordinance. That said, however, he acknowledges that there "is an affinity between the Christian community and the civil communities of free people" (44).

Back to the Beginning

"The first task of the church is not to make the world more just but to make the world the world." I should like to think, or at least hope, that you hear that sentence differently than when you heard it at the beginning of this chapter. I should like to think it a Barthian sentence. Rather than suggesting that the church by necessity or conviction must withdraw from the world, in fact the sentence is an invitation to engage the world. The sentence assumes, as Barth argued, that the "world" has been redeemed. The problem is that the world has no way of acknowledging that reality unless there is an alternative present. That alternative we call church.

That said, I confess I am not as convinced as Barth that his analogical method works in as straightforward manner as he seems to assume. It is not just that I find some of the analogies strained, but it is not clear to me that they are analogies. For example, I think it quite interesting that at times he uses the language of "translation" in relation to his exposition of the political implications of his theological claims just as often as he says he is developing analogies. It is also the case that some, if not most, of his analogies would not seem so obvious if there were not already existing democratic practices and institutions that guided his imagination. I worry that what Barth gives us is a theological justification for institutions that are already assumed to need no theological justifications.

I do not want to leave the impression that what Barth is doing when he develops these analogies is without merit. I suspect they only become a problem when the playfulness with which Barth developed them is lost. Barth seems to be saying, "If you think this analogy does not work, let me watch while you develop an alternative." What is important for Barth is not the particular analogies he develops but the Christological presumptions that make such analogies possible in the first place.

In that respect, however, I think many of Barth's analogies would have been stronger if they reflected the tension between the church and the world. If he had done that, then his account of the role of the church vis-à-vis the state would have been more concrete. At the very least, attention to the church/world duality would have forced Barth to assume a more determinative history of "the state." For example, it would have been quite interesting for Barth to talk not about "the state" but the nineteenth-century nation and state.

Todd Cioffi has challenged my suggestion in *With the Grain of the Universe* that Barth's ecclesiology is inadequate just to the degree he assumes that the church is too willing to let the world be the world. In particular, Cioffi directs attention to my worry that Barth is too ready to underwrite the liberal democratic state. Cioffi observes, as I have suggested above, that Barth's understanding of the church's support of democracy is not based on the truth of democracy as such but on the polity of the church. I certainly have no reason not to think that Cioffi is right about that, which raises the question of what Cioffi thinks is my problem.

I think, in a nutshell, that he thinks I overemphasize the role of the church because where Barth does Christology, I have an ecclesiology. Cioffi, therefore, thinks I have ignored key aspects of Barth's Christology.[13] Indeed, he thinks I have no Christology at all. I hope some of what I have done in these lectures might serve as a counter to that judgment, but I can at least direct attention to a fine book by Robert Dean entitled *For the Life of the World: Jesus Christ and the Church in the Theologies of Dietrich Bonhoeffer and Stanley Hauerwas* that argues that Christology is at the center of my work. It is, of course, humbling to be discussed alongside Bonhoeffer, but I should like to think Dean has it right. For, in his judgment, "Bonhoeffer and Hauerwas have come away from their engagement with Barth firmly convinced that God's self-revelation in Jesus Christ is the presupposition of all Christian thought and action."[14]

I think, however, that Barth's crucial insight is to be found in his contrast between church and state in terms of the coercive character of the state. Barth rightly emphasizes that there is a coercive character to the state in contrast to the church. We are not coerced to be a member of the church, but we are fated to be an American or Canadian. To be so fated is seldom noticed or theorized because it is assumed there is no alternative. But there is an alternative if Barth is right about the character of the church. That alternative is quite simple—the church keeps the coercive character of the state in check by telling the truth. This brings me back to the significance of language.

Wittgenstein observes in *Culture and Value* (41e) that "the truth can be spoken only by someone who is already at home in it, not by someone who still lives in untruthfulness, and does no more than to reach out towards it from within untruthfulness." What it might mean to be at home in the truth is not immediately evident, but surely if we are to know what being at home in the truth is, we will learn it in worship. Through repetition we will slowly come to acknowledge that this bread and wine are not "symbols" but reality.

The temptation is to think that in order to get a handle on not lying you need a theory of truth, which many worry no longer exists. This is not a new problem. The one we worship we believe was not only at home in the truth but was the truth. When a minor Roman official was told that this man was the one who had come into the world to testify to the truth, he asked the skeptic's question, "What is truth?" He received no answer. The ensuing silence indicates that the response to skepticism is not a theory but an exemplary life. Such a life, a life that is not only at home in the truth but is the truth, is the political reality that is our only hope in a world bent on violence.

There is much wisdom in Barth's analogies. I would not change any. But such imaginative tools only work if persons exist trained not only to say what is true but to live truthful lives. If such a people no longer exist, we are indeed in deep trouble. But by helping us speak again of God without apology Barth gave us skills necessary to recover a strong theological voice that does not betray the fragility of all speech but particularly speech about God. For that we should be rightly grateful.

4

Reinhold Niebuhr

AN INSIGHTFUL THEOLOGIAN

Reinhold Niebuhr One More Time

I am grateful to have this opportunity to write one more time on Reinhold Niebuhr. That I am ready to write one more time on Niebuhr is something of a surprise for me. A number of years ago I was asked to write an article on Niebuhr for a contributed volume on political theology. I declined by saying I have written often on Niebuhr and to write on Niebuhr again would give the impression I have a fetish about Niebuhr. So why have I accepted this invitation to write again on Niebuhr? I have done so because I want to counter the impression that I have nothing but negative judgments about Niebuhr. In fact, I admire Niebuhr as a person who often was capable of profound insights about the human condition.

Because I was quite critical of Niebuhr in my 2001 Gifford Lectures, some have drawn the conclusion that I have no positive regard for Niebuhr or his work. I still hold by the critique I made of Niebuhr in *With the Grain of the Universe: The Church's Witness and Natural Theology*. But those criticisms were just one aspect of the story I was trying to tell, that is, how William James, Niebuhr, and Karl Barth represent the great Gifford Lecture tradition. I thought that was a story worth telling.

It is true that in some ways I was more positive about James than about Niebuhr. In particular, I called attention to Niebuhr's master's thesis at Yale Divinity School, which was on James. In some quite distinct ways Niebuhr remained a "Jamesian" his whole life, but as I will suggest below, Niebuhr did not draw on the strongest aspects of James's work. I tried, not very successfully I might add, to show that Barth was more the pragmatist than Niebuhr. I thought, moreover, that was a compliment to Barth.

In my chapters on Niebuhr, I called attention to Niebuhr's claim that the "accumulated evidence of the natural sciences" convinced him that the realm of natural causation is more closed than the biblical world assumed. Accordingly, Niebuhr confessed that it is difficult to believe in the virgin birth or the "physical" resurrection of Christ.[1] For Niebuhr, God is the name that describes our need to believe that life has a unity that transcends the world's chaos and makes possible the limited order that can be achieved in our lives. Given that understanding of God, I suggested that Niebuhr's understanding of God is not that distinct from James's "more." Niebuhr translated James into what might be called Christian speech, and he did the translation so successfully that neither Niebuhr nor his many followers noticed that they had assumed a position that was anything but orthodox or even neo-orthodox.[2] I worried finally whether Niebuhr's anthropological method did not reproduce Feuerbach. I have not changed my mind about any of those worries.

Niebuhr could have exploited James's pragmatism in a more constructive manner. Niebuhr's master's thesis was primarily an attempt to provide an account of God given the developments in evolutionary science and metaphysics James represented. I suggested that one of the ironies about James's influence on Niebuhr was his failure to understand the significance of James's view that the implication of Darwin was not that a mechanistic metaphysics is unavoidable, but rather that after Darwin we can only understand that all that exists is but the result of absolute chance. For James we live, drawing on the title of Raymond Geuss's powerful book, in *A World without Why*.[3] Yet James also was a deep humanist. He thought as long as two creatures surrounded by an ocean of water were able to cling to a rock to avoid drowning there was some purpose present in the universe.

James's hope that some significance for human purpose is possible, however, was not the robust vision of Niebuhr. James and Niebuhr were equally committed to progressive causes, but Niebuhr had a passion that fueled a hope for justice that James did not possess. If there was anyone who exemplified what James identified as health-minded, it was Niebuhr. In many ways Niebuhr was a wonderful exemplar of James's stress on the significance of temperament.

There was another aspect of the James/Niebuhr relation I referenced in *With the Grain of the Universe* that has not drawn the attention for which I hoped. In my discussion of James's *The Will to Believe* I tried to show that James's shorthand version of pragmatism, that is, truth is what works, in fact is not James's position. For James truth is what happens to a sentence.[4] I take that to be a philosophical remark of great significance. Indeed, I suggested that Wittgenstein, who was a great admirer of James, could be interpreted as being in agreement with that sentence. I was trying to suggest, and I did it far too clumsily, that Barth's declaration that he "could only repeat himself" was one way to see how truth happens to what we say.

Niebuhr, of course, was not a philosopher so he would not have been on the lookout for the kind of questions in which I am interested. Actually, it is a very good thing Niebuhr was not a philosopher because if he had been a philosopher, he might have been hesitant to make the broad and often exaggerated claims in which he was the master. Though I am not in Niebuhr's league in that regard, I cannot deny that I learned from Niebuhr that an insight forcefully articulated can and should produce thought. Some have worried that some of the claims I have made about Niebuhr's work suggest that I do not think he was a Christian. That is certainly not what I think. Niebuhr was an extraordinary Christian to whom we owe much.

Niebuhr's general stance, however, was one that assumed that the church is just *there*. The church that was just there was primarily a conservative church both in its politics and theology. Niebuhr took as one of his tasks to challenge a too-satisfied Christianity. Yet such a project assumed a world in which mainstream Protestant Christianity seemed vital, safe, and secure. Like most liberal Protestant theologians, Niebuhr took as his task to help regain intellectual integrity for mainstream Protestant Christianity. Accordingly, he understood the fundamental claims of the Christian faith, claims such as the resurrection of Jesus, as "true myths" that appropriately express the fundamental paradoxes of life. Such myths are vital, but they are not to be taken literally.

I represent a very different theological agenda than Niebuhr, but I hope it is clear that I assume that Niebuhr was a more impressive Christian than I can ever pretend to be. I have suggested that Niebuhr's Christology and ecclesiology were "thin," but given his lecturing and preaching, in a sense he did not need to give an account of the church. He was the church. I am in quite a different place given that we can no longer assume that the church will just be there. Though I think that we still can learn from Niebuhr's theology and ethics, I also think what we have to learn is: *don't do it now the way he tried to do it then.*

Yet what I particularly admire about Niebuhr was the energy and imagination he brought to the work of Christian theology and ethics. He did not fear making the large claim that would on reflection need qualification. Yet he was able to do what many of us now think has to be done, that is, he was able to theologically story our existence. He quite literally could create, for those who heard him preach and lecture, a new reality. To suggest that Niebuhr's continuing significance is the energy and imagination that characterized his life and work may seem a backhanded compliment, but let me try to make the suggestion concrete by directing attention to one person's account of the effect Niebuhr had on him.

Langdon Gilkey's Testimony

We have a wonderful account of Niebuhr's energy and imagination, as well as the effect he had on those who heard and read him, by Langdon Gilkey. Gilkey's testimony is particularly significant because Gilkey went on to become a very distinguished theologian. That he did so has a great deal to do with Gilkey's encounter with Niebuhr when Gilkey was a young man. It was an encounter whose effect on Gilkey lasted throughout his life. We know that Niebuhr's effect on Gilkey lasted throughout his life because Gilkey describes the encounter in a book on Niebuhr he wrote late in life. Gilkey tells us he wrote the book, which was entitled *On Niebuhr: A Theological Study,* because Niebuhr's theology provides the possibility of a social realism to sustain a moral nerve. Gilkey thinks that extremely important because the same moral commitment in some people can lead them, when faced with the fact that the best we can do is achieve the lesser evil, to become cynical or despairing. Gilkey tells us he senses that a Niebuhrian perspective that can sustain the hard work of limited justice is still needed.[5]

Gilkey begins his book on Niebuhr by describing an early encounter he had with Niebuhr. Niebuhr and Gilkey's father were friends, so he had some impression as a child of Niebuhr by hearing his father speak of Niebuhr. But the decisive encounter occurred in 1940, just as Gilkey was soon to graduate from Harvard. Gilkey describes himself at that time as one of the confused young people who were distraught given the events in Europe and the Nazi victories. They were dispirited and filled with the despair of meaninglessness. He notes that he belonged to those generations brought up after World War I who had concluded that any war was useless and without justification. Their mind-set was, therefore, idealistic, and they inclined toward pacifism. Yet they were also a generation that had a passion for justice, having experienced the

Great Depression. Their lives were, therefore, filled with contradictions as they were unable to negotiate the tension between their commitments to peace and the need to strive for justice.[6]

The lives that embodied these confused ideals were made even more ambiguous by what Gilkey describes as the requirement their humanist morality demanded that they be virtuous individuals who sought to do good works. If a cause was just, then it was presumed that those supporting the cause should also be just. The world, however, proved to be a messy place, which made it hard to always know who were the good guys and who were the bad guys. The morality they assumed simply did not seem to know how to deal with the moral ambiguity they confronted. In effect their idealism blinded them to the complexity of the moral challenges they were facing.[7]

Into this bewildering and dispirited world came Reinhold Niebuhr. Gilkey's father informed Gilkey that Niebuhr was coming to Harvard to preach. Gilkey says he had by that time no idea who Niebuhr was, but out of respect for his father as well as curiosity he went. Gilkey describes his impression in a memorable way:

> The torrent of words, insights, and ideas that issued forth from that towering figure in the pulpit stunned me. This was not gentle and apologetic persuasion rounding out our "nice" ordinary experience with a moral and religious interpretation. This was from beginning to end a challenge to the assumptions of my sophisticated modernity. And that challenge came with a vividly new interpretation of my world. In fact a quite different viewpoint on everything was set before me, a viewpoint in my confused and deeply troubled "ordinary experience" suddenly clarified itself, righted, and became for the moment intelligible. There was here no appeal to an extrinsic authority: on the contrary there was an exceedingly realistic analysis of just the social situation that was troubling me. But this was an analysis structured by a framework, a wider "ontological" framework, which was very new to me ... To my astonishment Niebuhr identified his own utterly realistic appraisal of

the domestic and international situation (much more real than that of my philosophical mentors Bertrand Russell, John Dewey, or George Santayana) with what he called the "Biblical viewpoint."[8]

Gilkey reports that Niebuhr not only pointed out the "naïve optimism" of the humanistic and naturalistic philosophers he had treasured, but, even more, Niebuhr argued for the experimental validity as well as the moral strength of the "Biblical perspective." Gilkey tells us he felt overwhelmed. It was as if he had stepped into another space in which a new quality of light changed everything, making comprehensible what had been obscure. "In short," Gilkey tells us, "he opened up the possibility of a realism about social affairs that did not lead to cynicism, and yet, on the contrary led to a confidence in transcendence that supported a renewed and re-strengthened moral commitment."[9] Gilkey says he was by no means converted, but he was deeply intrigued.

But, of course, he was converted. Indeed, one could hardly wish for a more vivid conversion narrative. It is a narrative, moreover, that I am confident could be repeated by countless people who, like Gilkey, heard or read Niebuhr and had their lives transformed. Whatever one may think of Niebuhr's theology, his Christology or lack thereof, his understanding of the relation of love and justice, accounts like that of Gilkey are not to be overlooked or dismissed as youthful enthusiasm and hero worship. Gilkey's report is significant not only because he became Langdon Gilkey but because, as Gilkey says, Niebuhr opened up a new world for him by helping him see theologically the world in which his life was to play out. How could you not admire a person who could have such an effect on someone like Gilkey?

Why Niebuhr's Insights Matter

I think it was not accidental that Niebuhr was preaching when he turned Gilkey's life upside down. Of course, in general it is not always clear that you can distinguish Niebuhr's sermons from his more academic essays and books. I do not say that in criticism because I think it quite a good thing that Niebuhr's sermons and books were not markedly different from one another. I am sure Niebuhr had some idea that his sermons and his books and essays often could not be distinguished because he described the sermons in *Beyond Tragedy* as "sermonic essays."[10] The subtitle of that book is equally telling, namely, in those sermons he tells us he is exploring the complex subject of the "Christian interpretation of history."

I think the power of his sermons as well as much of his other work was due in large part to what I can only characterize as his ability to formulate insights that prove to be unforgettable. I have always thought that Niebuhr was so persuasive because he had the ability to illumine our lives with well-hewn insights. Indeed, I suspect that often readers and hearers of Niebuhr became Niebuhrians because they were attracted to an insight and assumed that you could not have the insight without his general theological position. I will suggest below, however, that the relations between many of his insights and his theology are more ambiguous than they seem.

Before developing that thought, however, I need to give some examples of what I am calling Niebuhr's insights as well as say something about what I take an insight to be. For example, consider this sentence from a sermon in *Beyond Tragedy,* a sermon entitled the "Transvaluation of Values": "The culture of every society seeks to obscure the brutalities upon which it rests."[11] Niebuhr could be giving expression to Hegel's observation that history is a slaughter bench, but the grammar of the insight is all Reinhold Niebuhr. The insight, moreover, expresses the main theme of the sermon, which is that every form of human eminence is subject to sin and self-destroying pride, which inevitably leads to civilizations being destroyed by the defects in their own virtues.[12]

Niebuhr's ability to sum up an argument by a telling insight I think reflects, as I suggested above, his extraordinary energy and imagination. It may seem odd to suggest that insights are the product of energy and imagination, but insights are no common thing. Bernard

Lonergan, for example, begins his extended examination of the character of insights by directing attention to detective fiction. Lonergan observes that readers of detective novels are often given all the clues they need to know who did it, but they often cannot spot the criminal. Lonergan notes that the reader needs no more clues to solve the mystery, yet they remain in the dark because to reach a solution is not the result of the apprehension of any one clue or even the memory of all the clues. Rather the discovery of "who did it" is a "distinct activity of organizing intelligence that places the full set of clues in a unique explanatory perspective."[13]

Niebuhr developed "a unique explanatory perspective" that allowed him to make "supervening acts of understandings." I have no doubt that he had the gift of insight not only because he was an intuitive person and thinker, but, just as important, because he refused to underwrite the sentimentalities so often associated with Christians who think being a Christian means they must be without judgment of others—for example, "when it is all said and done, we are all equally sinners." Niebuhr, whose insights, as I will suggest below, betray a person of remarkable practical wisdom, wrote to make idealists face the limits of the past by reminding them that the achievement of justice often comes through some suffering an injustice.

Abraham Heschel, Niebuhr's good friend, in his book on the prophets makes some remarks about the character of insight that are illuminative for Niebuhr's work. Heschel suggests that conventional people see the present in terms of the past, whereas people of insight think in the present. To be able to think in the present, Heschel suggests, requires an intellectual dismantling of the given that often creates a sense of dislocation. Insights are, therefore, accompanied by a sense of surprise because insights create a new way to see. It is a seeing, moreover, that is made possible through words. Heschel depicts the prophets as agents of insight just to the extent that they had insights that shattered indifference.[14]

Niebuhr's insights often seemed to correspond to Heschel's description of the insights of the prophets. Accordingly, it is assumed that Niebuhr's insights seem to be the outworking of his theology, but I think that must be carefully put. No doubt some of his insights seem to come directly from his theological reflections. For example, I have always thought his account of sensuality in *The Nature and Destiny of Man* to be Niebuhr at his best. He is particularly insightful, for example, in his account of drunkenness, which he suggests rather than being a desire to enhance the ego is in fact more likely to be an attempt to escape knowledge of ourselves.[15] He is equally interesting in his account of lust, which he describes as the attempt to lose ourselves by sinking into our bodies. According to Niebuhr, sensuality is the final form of self-love, which ironically takes the form of a "plunge into unconsciousness."[16]

The insights that constitute Niebuhr's account of sin as pride and sensuality make compelling reading. You cannot help but learn wisdom from Niebuhr, but that does not mean Niebuhr's account of sin is theologically determined. In *With the Grain of the Universe,* I suggested that sin was Niebuhr's way of doing natural theology.[17] By that I meant to indicate that Niebuhr did not worry that his understanding of sin was basically a natural theology. For all the insight that Niebuhr displays in his account of sin, he assumes that sin can describe human existence even if God does not exist. Niebuhr seems to forget that sin names alienation from God.

Probably Niebuhr's most famous insight is from *The Children of Light and the Children of Darkness:* "Man's capacity for justice makes democracy possible; but man's inclination to injustice makes democracy necessary."[18] This famous insight is quoted often but is seldom analyzed for the care Niebuhr put into its form. No doubt if he were writing today the masculine would not be so dominant. But the words he uses are quite specific. We have a *capacity* for justice but an *inclination* to injustice. That is a distinction Niebuhr knew was worth pondering, and ponder it he did not only in this book but in most of his political writing.

Niebuhr wrote *The Children of Light* at the height of the uncritical celebration of democracies at the end of World War II. He wrote hoping to cool the ardor for democracies after the end of war. I call attention to this book as well as the central image that shapes the book because I think they suggest Niebuhr's greatest strength—he was a man of extraordinary practical intelligence. That intelligence, moreover, was an expression of his willingness to say what he understood to be true even if doing so made him enemies he did not need.

Niebuhr the Man

Finally, I want to make clear how deeply I admire Niebuhr the man. He seemed to be tireless, often teaching a class with a suitcase by his side. Moreover, he seems to have done what is extremely difficult to do—he was not trapped by his fame or success. It seems clear that having married late, he had married a very strong woman who seems never to have been impressed with Niebuhr's academic and nonacademic success.

Finally, "after Niebuhr" I suspect few can imagine a theology that does not also address issues in political and social ethics, now that "social ethics" is assumed by many to be a subdiscipline of Christian ethics that no longer requires justification. Though some within the assumed subfield of social ethics are very critical of Niebuhr for being too "establishment," the various kinds of social ethics that are currently practiced can trace their being to Reinhold Niebuhr. I confess I find that result sobering.

Niebuhr will be forgotten. That is the destiny of us all. I suspect that is a thought he might have had along the way. But with a physical and intellectual energy few possess he made a difference when a difference needed to be made. Those of us who live in his wake are in his debt.

5

Karl Barth and Reinhold Niebuhr

THEIR DIFFERENCES MATTER

The Inevitable Conflict

Karl Barth (1886–1968) and Reinhold Niebuhr (1892–1971) were each larger-than-life individuals. Their writing alone is amazing in quantity and quality, but they were also engaged in political and societal life. One suspects that their presence would take up all the air in the room. They did not occupy the same rooms often, but in the room called Christianity—and that smaller room called Christian theology—they could make it difficult for the other to get sufficient air. They were men of enormous intellect and energy who, one would like to think, recognized something of themselves in the other.

It would seem they were destined to come into conflict. A date and place can be established when that conflict became public. It was in 1948 at the World Council of Churches meeting in Amsterdam. Prior to Amsterdam, Reinhold Niebuhr had occasionally written about Barth. The Barth he wrote about seems to have been Barth of the Romans. In these early articles he expressed high regard for Barth, though he worried about Barth's "absolutism."[1]

Barth clearly haunted Niebuhr, but I think it fair to say that Barth did not return the favor. He certainly had some acquaintance with Niebuhr, but Barth would have thought Niebuhr's theology "thin." In 1947 Niebuhr had come to Europe and invited himself to visit Barth in Bonn. Barth reports that Niebuhr's anticipated visit filled him with trepidation because, as Barth wonderfully puts it, he worried whether "we would sniff at each other cautiously like two bull mastiffs, or rush barking at each other, or lie stretched out peacefully in the sun side by side."[2] Barth does not say which description best characterizes their meeting, but he reports that they had a good conversation.

They may have had a good conversation in Bonn, but the difference between them exploded in Amsterdam. It will be the burden of the first section of this chapter to provide the background necessary to understand what happened at Amsterdam. I think that important because their differences continue to matter. Their disagreements are of historical interest, but because they continue to represent alternatives, particularly in theological ethics, which continue to shape the field, it is important to understand their differences. I do not want, however, to keep anyone in suspense—I think Barth usually had the best of the arguments between them.

Niebuhr first wrote about Barth in 1928 in an article entitled "Barth—Apostle of the Absolute," which was published in the *Christian Century*. Niebuhr began his article observing that for some time Barth had been seen as an important theologian but that it was difficult to say why Barth is significant because his books had not been translated, causing his work to appear fragmentary. Niebuhr expressed hope that might be changing because Douglas Horton had just translated Barth's *Word of God and Theology*.

In this early article Niebuhr gave a largely positive account of Barth. He noted, for example, that some considered Barth to be a fundamentalist because of the bombastic character of his Romans commentary. Niebuhr defended Barth from that charge by pointing out that Barth accepts the results of biblical criticism. As their differences over the years became more pronounced, Niebuhr became more sympathetic with those who called Barth a fundamentalist. I suspect Niebuhr never thought Barth was a fundamentalist, but he certainly did think Barth's theology was, in his word, obscurantist.

Early in Niebuhr's career he thought that Barth and he shared a similar critique of Protestant liberal theology. Niebuhr characterized Barth as a theologian who was rightly reacting against the subjectivism and relativism of liberal theology. He assumed, however, that Barth's criticism of liberal theology did not commit Barth to the view that Christian theologians over the centuries had not developed a better understanding of God. Yet Niebuhr expressed worries about Barth's stress on revelation, which he feared could lead to a regrettable absolutism. But Niebuhr thought Barth's Christology to be a promising way to express our alienation from God.

Niebuhr commends Barth for "reintroducing the note of tragedy in religion" because it is an antidote to the superficial optimism of most current theology.[3] Yet he worries that Barth's reassertion of the absolute in Christ pays too high a price for whatever advantage is gained. Niebuhr explains that for Barth it is not really the Christ-life that is the absolute but it is rather the "Christ-idea." Niebuhr, and he cannot be thinking of Barth's work other than the Romans, argues that Barth's theology is not at all interested in the peculiar circumstances of Christ's life. Niebuhr even suggests that Barth is not interested in the ethics of the Sermon on the Mount. What interests Barth, according to Niebuhr, is a "Christ idea" that may have little relation to the historical Jesus. But that leads Niebuhr to wonder, "How do we know that this Christ-idea is absolute and not subjective: we do not know."[4] Because we do not or cannot know, Niebuhr fears Barth is offering a dogmatically stated position that is without proof.

Niebuhr comments on this dogmatic strategy, suggesting that for Barth to so understand the role of the absolute is equivalent to the experience of justification by faith. Barth's account of justification, Niebuhr thinks, is promising because it suggests a dogma like justification may be true because it meets human needs. Yet Niebuhr argues that such an "abstruse" theology, a theology designed to escape relativism, in the end can do no more than result in a sorry victory. It is a sorry victory because, Niebuhr asks, how are we to know that the human need this kind of religion is designed to satisfy does not in the end satisfy a far too morbid conscience? Niebuhr speculates that the kind of morbidity that hangs over Barth's theology may reflect the sense of tragedy that World War I created in Europe and particularly in Germany, but that does not make it any the more attractive.

Niebuhr thinks Barth has had to pay far too high a price to make his position coherent. In order to defeat relativism, Barth's theology threatened to be quietistic. It is so because Niebuhr suspects that Barth is more concerned with the inner life than with project of advancing the progressive values of society. That Niebuhr could make such an argument indicates the mistaken view of many at the time that Niebuhr's stress on sin allied him with Barth's criticism of modern liberal views of social progress. Niebuhr, however, was quite clear that Barth did not give the appropriate reason for why Christians have an ongoing responsibility to work for a more nearly just society. Niebuhr acknowledges that Barth rightly thinks that history is the story of brutality, but Barthian pessimism can tempt some to "despair of history and take flight into the absolute which can neither be established upon historical grounds nor justified by any rational process, but can only be assumed and dogmatically asserted because it seems morally necessary."[5]

Niebuhr will sharpen these early arguments against Barth through a series of short but powerfully written articles. Quite understandably, given the confrontation at Amsterdam, many assumed that Niebuhr's critique of Barth was primarily against Barth's ethics. But Niebuhr was perhaps even more worried that Barth's theology would fail to meet the intellectual standards of the modern university. For Niebuhr the intellectual and the ethical aspects of the faith were closely interrelated, and he feared Barth met neither standard.

Niebuhr continued to develop his criticism of Barth in articles in the

Christian Century. In 1931 Niebuhr wrote an article entitled "Barthianism and the Kingdom" in which he continued to develop his criticism of Barth's "absolutism." He observes that the Barthians are very critical of present society but they fail to develop the grounds necessary to sustain their criticism. Niebuhr observes that Barth and his followers lack an adequate social ethic but given Barth's early socialism, that fact can go unnoticed. Niebuhr thought, however, that Barth and those influenced by him were giving up on efforts to improve society. Barth and his followers worry more about the pride and conceit that social actions may produce with the result that the salvation brought by Christ is betrayed.[6]

According to Niebuhr, it is crucial to see that the moral sensitivity and corresponding lack of social vigor and disdain for the historical that characterize the work of Barth and his disciples have the same source. That source is a stress on religious perfectionism. Niebuhr worries that when Barth's depiction of God, God's will, and the Kingdom of God are described in such idealistic and transcendent terms, nothing in history can match them. As a result, the distinction between good and evil is obscured, making impossible judgments about how, amid the ambiguities of history, relative goods can be achieved. Niebuhr's criticism of Barth increasingly takes on an extremely negative tone.

In a later article, "Barthianism and Political Reaction," that appeared in the *Christian Century* in 1934, Niebuhr developed this attack by suggesting that Barthians lack a passion for social justice. One of the reasons for that absence is Barthians' increasing recognition that no society exists without some degree of coercion. Yet their failure to support the underprivileged because such support entails coercion results in giving the privileged a free ride. Niebuhr confesses, as one who bears wounds from doing battle with a complacent liberalism, that the appropriation of Barth's thought by reactionaries tempts him to return to the liberal camp.

For the first time, however, Niebuhr makes an important qualification. He disavows any attempt to associate Barth's theology with the support of Hitler. He rightly identifies Barth as one of Hitler's most determined foes, and he expresses admiration for Barth's stance. Later, however, Niebuhr says he is astonished about Barth's letter to "a theological professor in Prague" in which Barth suggests that Czech soldiers have a Christian duty to kill Germans. Such a letter, Niebuhr thinks, exposes the contradictions in Barth's position, that is, Barth confuses relative political judgments with the unconditional demands of the gospel.[7]

Niebuhr returns to these issues in 1939 in an article in *Radical Religion* entitled "Karl Barth on Politics." Niebuhr provides an account of Barth's justification for his letter in which he seems to approve of Barth's characterization of Nazi politics as not just a political program but equivalent to a counterreligion to Christianity that promises a false salvation. Even though the Nazis describe their program as Christian, it is, Niebuhr argues, a religion diametrically opposed to Christianity. Niebuhr applauds Barth's claim that National Socialism must be opposed, but Niebuhr suggests that opposition means that Barth should acknowledge he has changed his position. Niebuhr argues that Barth's opposition to the Nazis means he is now ready to identify certain social strategies as required by the gospel. Niebuhr thinks Barth now holds a position not too different from his own. His only criticism is that Barth does not admit that he has changed his position.[8]

We have no evidence that Barth read or responded to any of Niebuhr's early criticisms of his work. The war and the struggle of the German church were all-consuming for Barth. One suspects that Barth, the primary author of the Barmen Declaration, would have found Niebuhr's suggestion that he had changed his understanding of the relation of Christianity and politics to be a profound misreading. After all it was Barth who had written in the Barmen Declaration: "As Jesus Christ is God's assurance of the forgiveness of all our sins, so in the same way and with the same seriousness he is also God's mighty claim upon our whole life. Through him befalls us a joyful deliverance from the godless fetters of this world for a free, grateful service to his creatures. We reject the false doctrine, as though there were areas of our life in which we would not need justification and sanctification through him."[9] The Barmen Declaration reflected Barth's refusal to understand the relation of the church and the civil community in terms of the two-kingdom duality shaped by the Reformation. That was and is an extraordinary development. It is not clear, however, that Niebuhr understood the significance of what Barth was doing. In particular Niebuhr did not seem to appreciate that Barth had called into question the Lutheran dualism between the order of creation and redemption.

Niebuhr was right to think that Barth's position was shaped by his eschatology, but he failed to understand that for Barth creation is an eschatological concept. As I suggested above, these matters came to a head at the founding assembly of the World Council of Churches meeting in Amsterdam in August 1948. There the difference between Barth and Niebuhr became dramatically clear. It is to that dramatic event I now turn.

Amsterdam

Eberhard Bush reports that Barth first said "no" when asked to give the speech that was to open the first assembly of the World Council of Churches (WCC). The assignment meant that Barth would need to read the four preparatory volumes that had been written for this event. However, he was urged to reconsider by theologians, particularly theologians in Eastern Europe, he had influenced. Barth agreed to give the opening address only to discover that the materials prepared for the assembly were written from a perspective that had been the subject of Barth's withering critique.

The assembly was gathered under the banner "Man's Disorder and God's Design." It was a slogan that Barth could not help but challenge. For Barth the order was backward. It is a profound mistake, Barth argued, for the WCC to begin speaking about the world's disorders in order to offer social and political ideals that they think might solve the world's problems. Rather, Christian speech about the world must begin with God's kingdom, "which has already come, is already victorious, and set up in all its majesty." Accordingly, the church must begin "with our Lord Jesus Christ, who has already robbed sin and death, the devil and hell of their power."[10]

Barth was not about to give those who had worked hard to develop materials for the WCC a free pass. He observed that the body of Christ only lives from and through the One who is wholly present to us, but he confesses that he is frightened by the fact that, in all the materials prepared for the Assembly, Jesus Christ has little or no work to do. It is as if God's providence, his already founded Kingdom, the accomplished reconciliation of the world, the presence of the Holy Spirit, and the triune God—his person, purpose, and glory—lay somewhere outside the circle envisaged under the theme of "Man's Disorder and God's Design."[11] Barth, no doubt with a sense of irony, suggested that "'God's design' does not mean something like a Christian Marshall Plan."

Barth develops his criticism of the papers prepared for the meeting by observing that many of the documents written for the meeting express worry that we may be entering a post-Christian era. Barth challenges that very way of understanding the task before the church, pointing out that the phrase "post-Christian" was first used by the National Socialists. But equally problematic is the assumption that some form of quantitative thinking, all calculation of observable consequences, all attempts to achieve a Christian world order, should determine the character of the witness to the sovereignty of God. The Christian task is first and foremost to point to God's kingdom. Christians have no Christian systems of economic or political principles to offer, but what they offer is a hope that is grounded in God's work in Christ.[12]

Barth concludes his address before the assembly by maintaining that in the face of the political and social disorder of the world, the task of Christians is to be witnesses and disciples of Jesus. To be such a witness means that Christians will have no problem having something to do. Christians have meaningful work to do because God has done the work that makes what Christians can do meaningful. Accordingly, the work Christians are called to do is freed from the desperate attempt to live lives that assume it is up to us to make up for what we fear God has not done. Barth thought that was exactly the presumption that had shaped the materials that set the agenda for the first meeting of the WCC.

Gary Dorrien reports that Barth was surprised that Niebuhr took strong exception to Barth's criticism of the slogan that was to shape the meeting, as well as to Barth's dissatisfaction with the prepared reports. That Barth was surprised, Dorrien suggests, may have been because Barth and Niebuhr in the United States were often linked under the unhappy designation of being "neo-orthodox" theologians. Barth hated that description, but Dorrien suggests he may have had the impression that he and Niebuhr shared the same critique of the liberal reformism that shaped the WCC preparatory materials. Yet Dorrien rightly observes that, for all of Niebuhr's criticism of the liberal presumptions that too often were moralistic, even supporting pacifism, he remained a product of the Protestant social gospel. Accordingly, Niebuhr was not only appalled by what he considered Barth's indifference to political challenges, but he was equally concerned by Barth's assertion that Christians have no business accommodating the gospel to modern scientific thought.[13]

Niebuhr's response to Barth's Amsterdam speech was entitled "We Are Men and Not God," and, like Barth's speech, Niebuhr's response was published in the *Christian Century*. Niebuhr began by duly acknowledging that Barth had been a powerful witness in the German church struggle against Hitler. But Niebuhr suggested that it might be the case that a theology constructed in the face of a great crisis in history may fail to make the discriminating judgments necessary for a responsible social ethic.[14] Niebuhr argued that Barth's insistence that Christians qua Christians have no economic or political principles to offer the world means that Christians can dispense with the principles of justice that "represent the cumulative experience of the race."[15]

With his usual rhetorical brilliance, Niebuhr suggests that Barth represents the German flight from responsibility by trying to extend the virtue of yesterday to cover current problems. As a result, Niebuhr argues that Barth's address encourages the German tendency to think of the church as an ark that provides a perpetual home on Mount Ararat, that is, a place above worldly battles. Niebuhr acknowledges that "Continental" theology is scholarly, the pinnacle of the Christian faith, which makes him feel that he is an inadequate critic. Yet he argues that Barth's theology requires correction because "it has obscured the foothills where human life must be lived."[16] Continental theology rightly reminded us that God is supreme and not men, but Niebuhr suggested that the wheel has come full circle, tempting Christians to offer a crown without the cross, a triumph without a battle, a faith without perplexity.

Barth responded to Niebuhr by focusing on Niebuhr's contrast of Continental and Anglo-Saxon theology. He challenged Niebuhr's characterization by observing that he knows some English-speaking theologians who belong to the "Continental type." Yet Barth does not deny that there is a difference in the two theological traditions and that difference is the Bible. Accordingly, Barth confesses all he was trying to do in Amsterdam was to say, as the Bible says, that God's plan of salvation has already come in Jesus Christ. It is from that viewpoint that we have a faithful understanding of the world's disorder.[17]

Barth was sure that Niebuhr had not understood him. So Barth even developed a list of such misunderstandings. For example, Barth said that the action of the church in the world ought not consist in the proclamation of theoretical principles, which earns him the mistaken criticism that he is only willing to fight the Devil when he has shown both horns. Barth argued that Christians should not fill the role of Atlas, for which he is mistakenly charged with being a cultural obscurantist who would have the crown without the cross. Some have even criticized Barth for his emphasis on the "otherness" of God, leading some to accuse him of being a dogmatic Lutheran who seeks to be free from all responsibilities. Barth, in particular, calls attention to the characterization that he is trying to secure a home by remaining in Noah's ark on Mount Ararat. Barth concludes in exasperation, pointing out that he is accused of all these failings even though for ten years he has been rebuked in Germany for bringing the gospel and the law, faith and politics, the church and democracy, into too close connection with one another.[18]

Niebuhr might well be forgiven for not understanding what Barth was suggesting about how the Christian witness to the state should be developed. Will Herberg's collection of Barth's extremely important essays on church and state had not been published. Those essays, "Gospel and Law," "Church and State," and "The Christian Community and the Civil Community," in fact constitute Barth's political theology. In particular, as I noted above concerning the Barmen Declaration, Barth's Christological reading of the power and status of the state was not understood by Niebuhr, or, put more charitably, Niebuhr does not seem to appreciate the significance of Barth's Christological understanding of the state.[19] Nor did Niebuhr seem to have any knowledge or appreciation of Barth's development in "The Christian Community and the Civil Community" of the analogies that could inform Christian political judgments.[20]

To be sure, if Niebuhr had known of those aspects of Barth's thinking about politics, he might have been even more dismissive of Barth's position. I suspect he would have found many of Barth's analogies arbitrary, but, even more troubling, Niebuhr would have had difficulty accepting Barth's Christological account of the state. As I noted above, Niebuhr had some understanding of Barth's eschatological perspective, but Niebuhr did not see the difference that made, and it did not become central to Niebuhr's concern with what he took to be Barth's shortcomings. In an odd way, in his understanding of the state, Niebuhr was closer to some forms of the Lutheran "two kingdoms" view than Barth.

George Hunsinger helps clarify what may have been the most determinative difference between Barth and Niebuhr on these matters when he observes that Barth, unlike Niebuhr, characteristically did not think in terms of the "real" and the "ideal" as alternatives. Yet that alternative was at the heart of Niebuhr's charge against Barth of absolutism. Niebuhr thought Barth's Christological politics was an ideal that could not be realized. Because the ideal could not be realized, Niebuhr assumed Barth must abandon the messy world of the political. That way of understanding Barth reflected Niebuhr's position about love as the absolute ideal that cannot be realized in the messy world of politics.[21]

Hunsinger points out, however, that Barth did not think in terms of real and ideal but rather in terms of the real and the unreal. Niebuhr's concept of the real in contrast to Barth's was grounded in his anthropology, which meant sin made love unattainable. By contrast, Barth's "reality" was theocentric, which means Barth thought that it is God who sets the terms for what is real. As a result, Hunsinger argues, Barth maintains that God's love in Christ establishes what is real, meaning that sin becomes unreal, making possible alternatives that otherwise would not exist.[22]

Amsterdam had been the most intense face-to-face interaction we know concerning the relation between Niebuhr and Barth. Niebuhr left Amsterdam with the view that Barth's influence had to be countered. He acknowledged that Barth's theology was shaped by "profound" interpretations of the biblical faith, but he worried that achievement might beguile some into accepting Barth's attempt to preserve what Niebuhr described as the purity of the faith.[23] Niebuhr even claimed that no Christian could argue with Barth's stress on the redemptive power of Jesus life, death, and resurrection, but the question that arose at Amsterdam was whether the conclusions Barth draws from that article of faith rob Christians of an appropriate sense of social and political responsibility.[24]

If Niebuhr was right in his summation of the events in Amsterdam, one can only conclude that there had been a massive failure in communication. We should not be surprised that such a failure happened because Barth forces a reconfiguration of how Christians think and act in a manner that Niebuhr was bound to think problematic.[25] Yet

Amsterdam was not the end of Barth's and Niebuhr's battles. The WCC meeting in Amsterdam had taken place against the backdrop of a changing world order. It is to be expected, therefore, that Barth and Niebuhr would find themselves in very different places with the rise of Communism.

Fellow Traveler?

The changed world in which the WCC assembly had taken place can be put in a very exact way—the Cold War had begun. Because Barth bore the title of being the great enemy of totalitarianism, many expected him to take a stance against the Communist regimes of Russia and Eastern Europe. However, his stance toward the Communist takeovers after the war was quite different than his opposition to the Nazis. Barth was clear that he was not about to become a cold warrior. At least he was not, as many did, in the name of democracy going to side with the United States against the Soviet Union. As a result of his refusal to take sides he was often accused of being anti-American.

Barth's refusal to join the anti-Communist movement became a serious point of contention as the Soviets tightened their grip on Eastern Europe and in 1956 with the uprising in Hungary. Emil Brunner wrote a forceful letter that asked Barth, given developments in Eastern Europe, why he had not, as he had in the German case, taken a stance against the Communist regimes. Brunner pointedly directed Barth's attention to Niebuhr, who had, like Barth, first refused to be an absolute opponent of Communism, but subsequently Niebuhr, like Brunner, had assumed a position of complete opposition. Brunner wondered if Barth simply did not think totalitarianism to be that much of a problem because Barth had not based his criticism of Nazi Germany on the grounds that Germany had become a totalitarian state. In a similar manner, Brunner suggests that Barth has failed to see the threat Communism presented because for unknown reasons Barth seemed to regard the countries of Eastern Europe in more friendly terms.

Barth replied to Brunner's criticism in *Against the Stream*.[26] Barth came straight to the point by responding to Brunner's question of how Barth could have roused Christians to oppose the Nazis but not the Communists. Barth answered by observing that the church at certain times is called upon to vindicate the faith in terms of certain historical developments, but the church must not concern itself with various "isms" that come and go throughout history. What must focus the church's attention are the actual historical realities as they are seen in the light of the Word of God. The church never acts "on principle," but rather judgments must be made one case at a time. That is why the church rejects all attempts to develop a political system.

Barth argues that from 1933 until the end of the war a reality confronted the church unlike that presented by Communism. That difference was that Hitler had the power and tried in many ways quite successfully to overwhelm the souls of the German people. Opposition to him was then a matter of life and death because the godlessness the Nazis represented was unqualifiedly evil. The Nazis were, therefore, more dangerous than the Communists because they presented themselves in the guise of a falsified Christianity. The Communists never pretended to be a form of Christianity. That difference between the Nazis and the Communists, Barth explained, is why his opposition to the Nazis is different than judgments about the Communists.[27]

I have called attention to this exchange between Brunner and Barth because it is the background of Niebuhr's last extended response against Barth. In 1957 Niebuhr wrote an article in the *Christian Century* entitled "Why Is Barth Silent on Hungary?"[28] Niebuhr begins the article praising Barth's stance against Hitler, but it is in some ways hollow praise. It is so because Niebuhr says it is now obvious that Barth's resistance to the Nazis was dictated by his personal experience with tyranny by the Nazis rather than required by his theology. Niebuhr makes that judgment even though he indicates he has read Barth's *Against the Stream,* which means he must have read the exchange between Barth and Brunner as well as papers Barth gave on his lecture tour of Hungary. If he had read Barth, I am sure he would have continued to disagree with Barth, but the disagreement would have been more productive.

Instead of calling attention to Barth's understanding of the difference Hitler represented, Niebuhr concentrates on Barth's response to the question of whether a Christian can cooperate with a Communist government. Barth answered that there will never be a time in which the state will exist in its pure form as an ordinance of God, nor will there be a time when the state that is a diabolical perversion of God's intention will exist. Barth, therefore, suggests that there may be some avenues open to Christians even in Communist states. Niebuhr, however, concludes from Barth's answer that Barth does not seem to think that a diabolical government has or will exist. Niebuhr wonders how a man as wise and robust as Barth could have come to such a false conclusion.[29] But it is not clear, given Barth's reply to Brunner about the difference between the Nazis and the Communists, that he in fact thought what Niebuhr attributes to him.

Niebuhr uses this characterization of Barth and, in particular, Barth's judgment about Hungary to expose what he takes to be the limits of Barth's theological method. According to Niebuhr, Barth simply lacks the resources for wise judgments for two primary reasons: (1) he is too consistently eschatological to justify the necessity of calculating how to achieve politically the lesser good; and (2) his approach to political and social problems is far too pragmatic. Interestingly enough, in support of these criticisms Niebuhr calls attention to Barth's suggestion that the totalitarian character of the Nazis was of a different order than the Communist brand. Niebuhr bluntly describes Barth's judgments about such matters as capricious.

Niebuhr ends his attack on Barth by suggesting that one could forgive Barth many things because he is a creative and imaginative theologian. We might even be ready to forgive arbitrary judgments about politics, although one could wish Barth studied the realities of political order more. But what, Niebuhr asserts, cannot be forgotten or forgiven is Barth's failure to confess that he was wrong about Hungary. Niebuhr observes that even Jean-Paul Sartre has disavowed what the Russians did in Hungary, and he sees no reason that Barth should not do the same.

As far as I know, Barth did not respond to Niebuhr's "Why Is Barth Silent on Hungary?" article. One has no way of knowing what Barth may have thought of Niebuhr, but I suspect he became less and less interested in Niebuhr's criticisms because he could not help but recognize that Niebuhr represented the methodological characteristics of Protestant liberal theology that Barth had claimed to have left behind. What is clear, however, is that the fundamental issues between Barth and Brunner were Christological.

The Differences Matter

In an incisive article entitled "The Lordship of Christ and the Gathering of the Church: Hauerwas's Debt to the 1948 Barth–Niebuhr Exchange," Brandon Morgan put the matter just right. He suggests that theologically Barth and Niebuhr inhabited different worlds. For Barth the care of the church and the care of the world were not a necessary burden for Christians to bear. Barth was about advancing the freedom of the church to be gathered according to Christ's reconciling work, which established his lordship over it in history. This makes possible the witness of the church, amid the world's disorder, to the true order established in Christ's cross and resurrection.[30]

Brandon observes that from Niebuhr's perspective this cannot help but appear theologically irresponsible. It is so because it seems to forego the task of securing relative justice by utilizing the use of power and even violence. That task means the church has no choice other than to act politically, but such action must often mean that at best the church can achieve a lesser evil. For Niebuhr, Christ stands on the edge of history, not, as Barth would have it, at its center.

Though Niebuhr might well have reservations about those who

now identify as social ethicists rather than Christian theologians and ethicists, in many ways he is the originator of that division. You do not need a church if you understand your task is to advocate in the name of justice for this or that cause. You can even follow Niebuhr and claim to be working out of a theological account of the human condition. For Barth the justice that Christians must pursue cannot be abstracted from the practice of the faith grounded in Christ's cross. This is a position that can only make Christian social and political engagements more difficult. I suspect Barth would have it no other way.

6

God and Alasdair MacIntyre

WITH A NOD TO BARTH

MacIntyre on Theology and Philosophy

There was a time when Alasdair MacIntyre was not a Christian. However, once he returned to the faith he did not keep his convictions as a Christian hidden. In the first chapter of *Whose Justice? Which Rationality?*, which was published in 1988, he identified himself as an Augustinian Christian.[1] He is, moreover, a Roman Catholic, which is an identity that earned him the scorn of philosophers such as Martha Nussbaum.[2] Some years ago at a gathering in the home of that great Thomist Ralph McInerny, MacIntyre told me he was an atheist, but he quickly added that he was a Roman Catholic atheist. He explained that only the Catholics worshiped a God worth denying.

In this chapter on MacIntyre's theology, I will touch on his transition out of and back into Christianity, but I will try to avoid any psychologizing of that process. MacIntyre is a philosopher, and his reasons for being a Christian are philosophical. I am not suggesting that philosophy excludes what might be termed personal factors in being a Christian or an atheist, but, as will become apparent in what follows, for MacIntyre it is philosophical considerations that have played a decisive role in his being a Christian.

To suggest, as I just did, that this is a chapter on MacIntyre's theology can be quite misleading because MacIntyre is adamant about his understanding of the relation of theology and philosophy. He forcefully insists that he is not a theologian. The task of theology is a rational task, but theology is inquiry on revealed truths that can only be acknowledged by faith.[3] That he does not "do" theology is significant given his strong distinction between theology and philosophy. Yet I will try to show that the relation between philosophy and theology in his work is more complex than his strong declarations about the independence of philosophy and theology.

For example, in the extremely informative prologue to the third edition of *After Virtue,* MacIntyre notes that when he wrote *After Virtue* (1981), he was an Aristotelian but not yet a Thomist.[4] He explains that his transition to Thomism was the result of his judgment that in some respects Aquinas was a better Aristotelian than Aristotle. In particular MacIntyre reports that he learned from Aquinas that his attempt to give an account of the human good purely in terms of practices, traditions, as well as the necessity of a narrative unity of human lives was inadequate without a metaphysical grounding. Aquinas provided such an account by showing that our agency depends on an end to which we are directed by our specific nature. MacIntyre acknowledges that he was in his early work close to Aquinas's position on agency, but it was his study of Aquinas's argument for a supreme good that made all the difference in why God matters.

MacIntyre realized that his understanding of the relation of being and the good was the fundamental metaphysical presupposition that shaped Aquinas's arguments for God's existence in question 5 of the *Summa theologiae.* According to MacIntyre, Aquinas rightly assumed that no revelatory knowledge is necessary to sustain such an understanding of the existences of a supreme goodness. He therefore argues that his account of the autonomy of philosophy is consistent with Aquinas's understanding of philosophy.

I have no doubt that MacIntyre is right that there are some passages in Aquinas's vast work that may suggest that philosophy is an independent discipline, but when Aquinas goes about his business, he does not seem to make a strong distinction between philosophy and theology. At the very least, Aquinas's emphasis on charity as the form of the virtues, which admittedly makes the status of the moral virtues ambiguous, would seem to make a strong distinction between philosophy and theology problematic.[5] Charity is not just the form of the virtues, it is the transformation of our knowledge of the way things are.

That MacIntyre disavows any attempt to do theology means he seldom makes use of any particularistic theological concepts. Jesus is seldom mentioned. Yet from time to time he will say something clearly theological. For example, in a wonderfully entertaining lecture entitled "What Has Christianity to Say to the Moral Philosopher?," he seems to complement his account of the end for which we were created with the contention that "there is in the end, on the Christian view, one and only one true story to be told about every moral agent, a story of how one loses one's life or gains it, of how one does or does not fail oneself and others."[6] To be sure he identifies this as "the Christian view," but if true, which I certainly take to be the case, such a claim seems hard to sustain without theological claims playing a more decisive role for our calling to live as followers of Christ.

As far as I know, MacIntyre's most extended set of theological reflections are in the lecture entitled "Catholic Instead of What?" that was given at a conference by the Center for Ethics and Culture at Notre Dame in April 2014. In that lecture he observed that we need the Jesus of the New Testament, who is most historically depicted in the work of N. T. Wright, if our lives are to manifest what it means to be Christian. But Wright's work is not sufficient in itself if Jesus has not and does not continue to speak through the apostles and bishops of the Catholic Church. He then makes some extremely insightful remarks about the importance of prayer for the sustaining of a Catholic culture.

It is not clear to me how MacIntyre would understand the status of these reflections, but I am sure he would not think he needs to change his mind about the relation of philosophy and theology. I suspect one of the reasons MacIntyre is intent to maintain a strong distinction between theology and philosophy is because of his resistance to reductive explanations of his position. In an interview with Giovanna Borradori, he is asked if it is true, as some of his critics suggest, that his more recent philosophical positions are a hidden reassertion of Christianity. MacIntyre responded, "It is false, both biographically and with respect to the structure of my beliefs."[7] MacIntyre continues by explaining that what he now believes philosophically he came to believe before he reacknowledged the truth of Catholic Christianity. He was able, he observes, to respond to the teachings of the church because he had "already learned from Aristotelianism both the nature of the mistakes involved in my earlier rejection of Christianity, and how to understand aright the relation of philosophical argument to theological inquiry. My philosophy, like that of many other Aristotelians, is theistic; but it is as secular in its content as any other."[8] In this context MacIntyre is clearly using the designation "secular" in a positive sense to suggest that Christianity by its very nature produces a world it need not control. Again I have no reason to doubt MacIntyre's account of his position, but I think his understanding of the relation of theology and philosophy is actually more complex than his response to Borradori suggests.

His most developed account of the relation of philosophy and theology is in *God, Philosophy, Universities: A Selective History of the Catholic Philosophical Tradition*. There he argues that philosophy "cannot provide us with adequate knowledge either of God or ourselves. What it can do is to give us sufficient reason to reject those philosophical conclusions that are at variance with the Catholic faith."[9] But he also suggests that theology necessarily touches on as well as uses philosophical concepts to do its work, which means philosophers have the duty of making theologians philosophically responsible. Therefore it is important that theologians receive a good philosophical education if they are to do well their work as Christian theologians.

Yet it is also the case that the church has a stake in the philosophers doing their proper work as philosophers. If, as MacIntyre argues, the philosopher's task is to discover and formulate timeless truths, then philosophers must always be in the process of renewing philosophy in part by revisiting its history. If philosophers fail in that task, it is in the church's compelling interest to sustain a philosophical inquiry that does so. It is, moreover, the case that, though reason has its own distinctive way of approaching the mystery of God's existence, God's self-revelation to Israel and in Jesus Christ does not make the philosophical task redundant.[10] That which is revealed provokes and elicits new questions by making us aware of aspects of our existence that may be unavailable to philosophy but, once made known, it is the task of philosophy to explore. The work of the philosopher and the theologian should, therefore, be complementary.[11]

MacIntyre may have presumed this understanding of the relation of philosophy and theology early on, but it was the publication of *Fides et ratio* that produced what I take to be this more complex and nuanced account of the role of philosophy for Christian theology.[12] Before developing his understanding of the kind of philosophical work he thinks is important for sustaining Christian convictions, I need to provide some history of MacIntyre's early identification with Christianity as well as his reasons for a time of not identifying as a Christian. For it is only against that background that we can appreciate how he understands the relation of the philosophical work required by Christianity and the social and political significance of the church in modernity.

MacIntyre on MacIntyre's Account of Christianity

From the beginning of his work as a philosopher MacIntyre has had a passionate interest in Christianity. His offhand remarks about this or that Christian theologian suggest he has read and continues to read Christian theologians from the past such as Augustine and Aquinas, as well as recent work done in New Testament by people like N. T. Wright. Of course he has extensive treatments of Augustine and Aquinas in

Three Rival Versions of Moral Enquiry: Encyclopedia, Genealogy, and Tradition, but his reflections on what might be considered theological matters are often to be found in hard-to-find occasional essays—some still unpublished.[13] So I will need to ask your patience as I try to provide an account of MacIntyre's theological judgments, as well as his own understanding of the intellectual developments that have made him a faithful and fierce Roman Catholic.

In the 1970 edition of *Metaphysical Beliefs,* a book to which Mac-Intyre, Stephen Toulmin, and Ronald Hepburn each contributed, Mac-Intyre wrote a preface explaining why a book first published in 1959 should be republished. In his preface to the new edition he observes that the writers were clearly captive to the intellectual climate that prevailed at the time. Ayer's *Language, Truth, and Logic* represented the general stance of many philosophers who assumed that some account of logical positivism was a given. Accordingly, metaphysics was no longer considered to be a fit subject for philosophy. But MacIntyre observes that the work of Wittgenstein and Austin signaled that new possibilities were afoot. The latter developments were particularly important for the position MacIntyre developed in his chapters in the book, which he characterized as centered on the claim that "religion is a specific 'form of life' with its own criteria, its own methods of settling its own questions."[14]

MacIntyre so characterized the position he took in the book in order to disavow what he once advocated. He explains that criticisms by Hepburn forced him to see that his earlier Wittgensteinian-inspired position could not account for the character of religious faith about such matters as the persistence of evil. For if Christian theologians believe the persistence of evil is prima facie evidence against belief in God which must be answered, then theologians assume that such a belief is factual in a perfectly ordinary sense. That means the judgment that religious convictions have a particular logic that is unique to them is clearly false. MacIntyre draws the conclusion, therefore, that his attempt to give an account of Christianity that makes belief irrefutable cannot help but result in the cost of making those same beliefs perfectly vacuous. Thus the view that belief cannot argue with unbelief but can only preach to the latter has the effect of making Christian belief irrational, false, and dangerous.[15]

MacIntyre had developed this perspective in an article in 1964 entitled "Is Understanding Religion Compatible with Believing?" He argued that what is at stake between the skeptic and Christian is not only the character of the difference between belief and unbelief but the issue of belief itself. For the Christian to refute the skeptic they must provide an alternative account of intelligibility, but that cannot be done given the social context in which arguments must be developed. Thus MacIntyre claims that understanding Christianity is incompatible with believing in it. This is not because Christianity is necessarily vulnerable to skeptical objections, but "because its peculiar invulnerability belongs to it as a form of belief which has lost the social context which once made it comprehensible."[16] I call particular attention to this formulation of what he takes to be the challenge before Christianity because it suggests how MacIntyre's Marxism plays a role in his understanding of how the social and political challenges facing Christianity have the effect of making Christians unintelligible to themselves.[17]

For example, MacIntyre responds to the objection that Christianity is still viable in America by acknowledging that churches were the historical vehicle of American values of equality and achievement. But this was a mixed blessing because American religion survived industrial society only at the cost of becoming (in the bad sense) secular.[18] By trying to provide a moral code for Christianity in America, the church lost what made it Christian. What happened to the church in America is but an outworking of the tension in Christianity between its attempts to become a societal morality for anyone/everyone when the ethic of the early church is one that only makes sense for a small community whose members are separated from the wider society.[19] Troeltsch could not have put it better.

MacIntyre argues that attempts to defend Christianity in terms amenable to a secular culture had the effect of making Christian convictions unintelligible. As a result, he found it difficult to continue to think of himself as a Christian. In the 1995 introduction to *Marxism and Christianity* he explains that Christianity had become problematic for him because of his presumption that the terms that determine how theological claims were to be understood were best expressed in the theology of Karl Barth. Yet he came to the conclusion that Barth could not provide an adequate account of the moral life. He acknowledges that because he mistakenly assumed that this defect in Barth's theology was also a defect in Christianity as such, he could no longer identify as a Christian.[20]

What remains unclear, however, is exactly what MacIntyre understood to be an "adequate account of the moral life" as well as why such an account was, he thought, missing in Barth. In his interview with Borradori in which he explains his alienation from Christianity, he returns to the account he gave in the preface to *Metaphysical Beliefs* concerning his attempt to blend Wittgenstein's notion of form of life with Barth's theology. He refers to Hans Urs von Balthasar's criticisms of Barth, which convinced him that in crucial ways religious language and practices are inseparable from nonreligious metaphysical, scientific, and moral claims. He observes Barth had no way to meet those philosophical demands. He acknowledges that his early views about Wittgenstein were mistaken in terms of what Wittgenstein meant by "forms of life," but he continued to claim that his criticisms of Barth were on the mark.[21] I will raise some questions about that below because I will suggest that MacIntyre had and continues to have more in common with Barth than he thought at the time.

MacIntyre's Critique of Liberal Theology

I can explain this last remark by calling attention to some of the judgments that MacIntyre and Barth share. Both had disdain, a word far too soft to characterize their views, for liberal accounts of Christianity. Their worries about theological liberalism are not necessarily the same, though they are closely interrelated. Barth's concerns might be characterized as more methodological because of his focus on the anthropological starting point of the theological liberal enterprise, whereas MacIntyre's concerns have more to do with his criticisms of the accommodated character of liberal Christianity. The emphases are different, but they are also obviously interconnected.

It is useful to attend to MacIntyre's worries about liberal Christianity because his understanding of Christianity often is more explicit when he is criticizing theological liberals. That he was originally attracted to Barth says a great deal about his understanding of Christianity because I suspect one of the reasons MacIntyre was attracted to Barth, particularly the Barth of the Romans commentary, was their shared disdain for attempts to make Christianity amenable to some of the destructive presumptions of modernity, such as the compartmentalization of our lives that makes the acquisition of the virtues even more unlikely.

Barth matched MacIntyre's disdain for what he called "platitudinous emptiness of liberal Christian moralizing, whether Protestant or Catholic." Such moralizing MacIntyre associated with theologians such as Bultmann, Robinson, and Tillich, who he argued were trying to translate and disguise in a theological idiom what are essentially secular presuppositions.[22] By calling such a project "secular," MacIntyre was not paying theologians bent on such an endeavor a compliment.

Like Barth, MacIntyre will have nothing to do with such a project. But his reasons for rejecting attempts to make Christianity compatible with modern liberalism are not necessarily the same as Barth's. To be sure, like Barth, MacIntyre has no use for mainstream Protestant liberalism. MacIntyre's objections, however, are much more informed by his Marxism than Barth's more straightforward theological judgments against his former teachers. Given Barth's long-held socialist convictions, I cannot help but wonder why MacIntyre thought Barth had an inadequate ethic. At least it is hard to know what MacIntyre finds lacking in Barth if "ethics" names the development of a response to capitalism.

Of course, socialism and Marxism are not the same, but they have a great deal in common. In *Marxism and Christianity,* a book MacIntyre wrote when he was not yet thirty, MacIntyre was intent to show that Marxism and Christianity had much in common. In particular neither have any time for liberal political and economic arrangements. Both Marxism and Christianity share the judgment that liberalism is a system that robs people of any purpose necessary to sustain hope. MacIntyre observed that Marxism and Christianity, in quite different ways, are bent on rescuing individuals from insignificance by showing how the individual can have a role in a world-historical drama. In that respect, however, MacIntyre suggests that Christians have a resource that Marxists lack, that is, the conviction that such purpose is not an illusion but is liturgically enacted by Christians.[23] MacIntyre's rejection of Marxism as a state system and his attempt to offer an alternative by focusing on small communities capable of forming virtuous people could be seen as an expression of a Barthian alternative.

MacIntyre's appeal, however, to the narrative character of existence enacted liturgically suggests that his criticism of theological liberals draws on a richer account of Christian practice than is immediately evident in his work. As I noted above, MacIntyre adamantly insists he is first and foremost a philosopher. He thinks it theologically important that philosophers disavow any ambition to be a theologian or to do theology. So he is extremely careful not to appear as though he is making theological judgments. But he clearly has schooled himself in Christian theology. He knows classical Protestant liberals like Schleiermacher and Troeltsch, but he seems more interested in Bultmann and Tillich. The latter are the subject of his withering critique in his 1967 Riddel Memorial Lectures at the University of Newcastle. In these lectures, which were published as *Secularization and Moral Change,* MacIntyre developed some of his most astute criticisms of liberal theology.

In particular he draws on his sociological insights to illumine the dead ends in which Christianity now finds itself. He observes that one of the central claims of Christianity has been its ability to incarnate itself in different forms of social life, which gives life meaning it would otherwise not have. But MacIntyre argues that the secular life of postindustrial societies no longer is able to give life the meaning that Christianity had supplied in the past. Christianity is now shaped by a secular (in the bad sense) world—even making such a world constitutive of its own life. As a result, he suggests that the claims of Christianity are rendered unintelligible by the actual history of modern society. Theologians have tried to respond to the challenge of the loss of Christian substance by making Christianity at home in such a world, but in the process they have robbed Christianity of any distinctive theological and political content.[24]

MacIntyre focuses on Tillich as the exemplification of this process. Tillich, according to MacIntyre, took as his fundamental project to explain God in terms intelligible to the modern world. To do so, Tillich left behind the metaphysics of Scholastic Catholicism because he judged such a position to be no longer relevant in the modern world. As an alternative, Tillich explains, what Christians mean by God is that God is the "name of man's ultimate concern." Such a suggestion, MacIntyre judges, may be an affective appeal against modern cynics and trivializers, and it might make entertaining sermons, but it is still the case that Tillich's "theism is merely a familiar form of atheism baptized with a new name."[25]

MacIntyre had made similar observations in 1969 in the book with Paul Ricoeur entitled *The Religious Significance of Atheism*. As a way to explain why the theism versus atheism debate has become culturally marginal, MacIntyre made the memorable judgment that "theists are offering atheists less and less in which to disbelieve. Theism thereby deprives active atheism of much of its significance and power and encourages the more passive atheism of the indifferent."[26] Theologians have apologetically resorted to a theological strategy that has tried to save what is thought to be essential to Christianity by distinguishing the kernel of Christian theism from the outmoded husk. As a result, Christianity has been robbed of its theistic content. For example, Bultmann's project to demythologize the gospel resulted in making Jesus an early anticipation of Heidegger. The desire of Protestant liberals to find a ground for believing in the truth of the gospel independent of the truth of Christian orthodoxy ends up making Christianity unbelievable. In particular, such strategies cannot account for the significance that orthodox Christianity has ascribed to Jesus.[27]

MacIntyre, like Barth, thinks the most devastating criticisms of positions like Bultmann's and Tillich's were not made by Christians but by Feuerbach (and Nietzsche). Feuerbach did not deny that theological language had a referent, but that referent turned out not to be God but rather the projections of a finite humanity against the reality of death. The only difference between Tillich and Feuerbach is that the theism in which Feuerbach disbelieved became the theism in which Tillich believed. Such theologies MacIntyre judges to exemplify the alleged disease they sought to cure.[28]

The disease that infected liberal theological proposals is the inability to engage the fundamental questions raised by our finitude. In *Secularization and Moral Change,* MacIntyre observes that when we move away from the sophisticated theologies of Tillich, there is a feature of Christianity that is very important to the naïve believer that theologians like Tillich do not adequately address, that is, how to sustain hope in the face of death. Yet Christianity still has a hold on many because it does sustain a hope in the face of death. Contemporary theologians say little theologically about death because they have accepted naturalistic accounts of our finitude. That hell and purgatory are no longer subjects of theological reflection is an indication that theologians have lost any basis for being taken seriously. Thus MacIntyre's judgment that we cannot do with Christianity in the modern world, but neither can we do without it because we have no other vocabulary to raise questions about how to live in the face of death.[29]

MacIntyre on the Catholic Philosophical Tradition

I have suggested that we have intimations of MacIntyre's theological convictions through his criticisms of what is essentially the Protestant liberal tradition. He clearly stands in the tradition of orthodox Christianity, but he does not think that tradition requires conflating the distinction between faith and reason, or philosophy and theology. In fact, Catholics rightly believe—or should believe—that philosophical arguments can provide responses to critical questions about what Christians believe they have been given through revelation. His most extended account of Catholic philosophy is in his book *God, Philosophy, Universities: A Selective History of the Catholic Philosophical Tradition*. One might think the phrase "Catholic philosophy" suggests a permeable relation between philosophy and theology, but MacIntyre does not relent because he argues that the Catholic tradition maintains that philosophy is, as he said earlier, secular.

MacIntyre begins *God, Philosophy, and Universities* by observing that Jews, Christians, and Muslims share a common understanding of God. For all three faiths God is necessarily One, that is, there is only God, and the God that is is One. MacIntyre seems to take this to be a grammatical remark that rightly maintains that if God is understood in any other way, then the god so conceived could not be the God of the three faiths. That God—that is, the God of Jews, Christians, and Muslims—necessarily exists in a manner that means there can be no other being that can set limits to the exercise of God's powers.[30] God so conceived exceeds our understanding, which means the words we use to address God must be extended "so that we no longer understand what we mean when we talk about God to the same extent and in the same way that we do in our speech about finite beings."[31]

Theistic belief, however, is not just the belief that such a being exists with the attributes just described. Some might acknowledge such a being exists but think they can remain indifferent to the existence of such a being. But to assume an attitude of indifference is to give up on the logic of Christian belief. For to believe God exists, MacIntyre argues, "is to believe that there is a being that affects all my relationships in a manner that affects everything that I do or might value."[32]

MacIntyre, in effect, argues that this puts the burden of proof on the atheist. He comes close to making this claim explicit in a 1998 paper entitled "Three Kinds of Atheism." MacIntyre argues that the mistake made by theists in conversation with atheists is to accept the atheist's presumption that God is an inferred entity. But the God in which the theist believes is a being that is present in encounters appropriate to such a being—such as prayer. Such an encounter the theist believes makes a decisive difference in how all that is should be regarded. The metaphysical implication that follows is that God's existence is the condition of "there being any genuine explanations."[33]

MacIntyre is well aware that the argument he is developing about God's necessary existence harkens back to Anselm's ontological argument. According to MacIntyre, Anselm rightly saw that God could not not exist. Having made that crucial move, Anselm then rightly argued that the God that we have in our minds must exist in reality. Such a God must exist in reality because if God does not exist in reality, then God could not be a being than which none is greater. But if we could conceive of a being greater than God, then we would be caught in a contradiction. Accordingly, we must reject the possibility of God so understood as not existing.[34]

MacIntyre reviews the familiar arguments against Anselm's position such as the common observation that existence cannot be a predicate. MacIntyre acknowledges the power of that objection but observes that such a criticism works because Anselm's argument has been abstracted from the faith in God that animated Anselm's life and argument. MacIntyre acknowledges that it is perfectly legitimate for philosophers, as they often have, to consider Anselm's argument abstracted from the theological frame that Anselm presupposed, but to do so is to miss the work it can do for unbeliever and believer alike. What Anselm's argument successfully does for theists and atheists is not to demonstrate the existence of God; rather, what is demonstrated is "the elusive character of the concept of God."[35]

MacIntyre ends *Ethics in the Conflicts of Modernity* noting that the completion of life consists in our persistent moving toward the best goods we know, which means some further good is always presupposed. Inquiry about such goods entails political and ethical inquiry, but MacIntyre suggests such inquiry must finally come to an end; that is where natural theology begins.[36] By making that the last sentence in the book, MacIntyre seems to want to leave the reader wondering what he could mean by natural theology, but in fact what he has done in *God, Philosophy, Universities* is a kind of natural theology. At least it is a kind of natural theology that MacIntyre associates with Newman.[37] Somewhat ironically it is also a natural theology that Barth might not have found so objectionable.

Consider, for example, this quotation from Barth's *Anselm*: "The Existence of God is not only unique but it is the sole existence which is real and ultimate, the very basis of all other existences and therefore just because of that also the only existence which in the strict sense can be proved."[38] Barth was, of course, the sworn enemy of all natural theologies, but it is remarkable how similar Barth and Aquinas seem to be in terms of how the tricky word "existence" works when we talk of God's existence. MacIntyre's account of natural theology is not an attempt to develop a knockdown argument but rather to show the conditions for the possibility of talk about God. In a similar manner, one can read Barth as struggling to know how to say what we say when we say God.

Where the Rubber Meets the Road

Barth had more to say about God than can be said by natural theologians because what Barth had to say was that Jesus has always been the elected one. After all, Barth was a theologian. But MacIntyre also has more to say about God as he spells out the implications for believer and unbeliever alike of the metaphysical claims about God's existence. *God,*

Philosophy, Universities was published in 2009. In 2011 MacIntyre developed what he meant by "the elusive character of the concept of God" in an article entitled "On Being a Theistic Philosopher in a Secularized Culture." It is not accidental that this was an address before the American Catholic Philosophical Association and was published in the *Proceedings of the ACPA*. He begins the article with the observation that it is assumed that the disagreement between theists and atheists is about the existence of God, but that is to understand the disagreement from an atheist's point of view. By contrast, the theist understands the disagreement to be about everything. It is so because "to be a theist is to understand every particular as, by reason of its finitude and its contingency, pointing toward God. It is to believe that, if we try to understand finite particulars independently of their relationship to God, we are bound to misunderstand them."[39]

MacIntyre develops the claim that what is at stake between atheists and theists is not the question of God's existence but rather the contrast between God's presence and absence, between occasions when God is manifest in and through particulars and when God does not seem present at all. MacIntyre makes clear he is not saying that all arguments about God's existence or nonexistence are pointless, but that such arguments are not to reassure someone that God exists. Rather they are meant "to exhibit the groundlessness of atheism."[40]

By the "groundlessness of atheism" MacIntyre means the presumption that if God did not exist, there would be only finite and contingent particulars. Such a chain of causes might be infinite, but the chain would still be finite, which is but a way to say that if God did not exist, there would have been nothing. In particular, if God did not exist, there would have been no atheist. MacIntyre observes atheists may regard such a response to be a cheap trick that theists use to maintain the presumption that belief in God is necessary to sustain public institutions. In response, MacIntyre calls attention to J. H. Newman's observation that the political establishment of the church has always been bad for the church. So theists should side with atheists for political arrangements that do not give special status to the church and thus give legitimacy to a variety of voices.[41]

MacIntyre addresses the widespread view that in our secularized society explanations and understanding are assigned to the natural and social sciences. Thus the atheist's view that every event or state of nature can be explained by these sciences. The theist has no reply to this strategy as long as explanation is understood in atheists' terms. What such a view fails to acknowledge is that every attempt to account for what happened or how it happened will require a further narrative. Thus contemporary physicists' understanding of the universe has a place for hadrons, leptons, bosons, for strong and weak forces, but it has no place for physicists or for any other intentionally informed agent. MacIntyre concludes that if physics sets the epistemological conditions of truth, then it is difficult to understand the existence of physicists—much less God.[42]

MacIntyre develops this argument by commenting on Dostoevsky's comment that if God does not exist, then everything is permitted. He observes that Dostoevsky was not saying that atheists are free from all moral constraints. Rather, what Dostoevsky was saying is that if atheism is true, then there is no type of action, no matter how horrifying, that some would nonetheless find reasons to perform. What Dostoevsky was predicting was not that given atheism there would be no reason to stand against the crimes as wicked as Auschwitz. Rather, he was predicting that crimes would be done in the name of lesser evil by seemingly good people, such as the bombing of Hiroshima. The logic of such justifications can only be exposed as never-to-be-done evils on theistic grounds.[43]

Without calling attention to what he is about in these arguments, and I think they deserve the description "argument," MacIntyre has developed quite interesting modes of natural theology, as well as an account of natural law. He has, moreover, written extensively on the latter in a paper entitled "Intractable Moral Disagreements" in which he argues that Aquinas's account of the precepts of the natural law provides the most satisfying account of moral disagreement.[44] In a reply to his critics, MacIntyre acknowledges that his account of natural law commits him to holding that practical reason rightly understood provides everything required for the moral life independent of any theological ethic.[45]

Yet just as MacIntyre noted that Anselm assumed the power of his argument for God's existence presumed faith in God, as well as a life of prayer, I cannot help but wonder if natural law does not require, particularly when the virtues are introduced, theological display. I have it on good authority that someone well versed in Aquinas's understanding of natural theology and natural law might be sympathetic to such an observation. I am, of course, referring to MacIntyre, who hints that this might be the case in an "Address Delivered at the Inauguration of Paul Joseph Philibert, O.P. as President of the Dominican School of Philosophy and Theology in 1987." In this address MacIntyre draws on Aquinas to maintain that the universal principles of the natural law are necessary to make the particulars of the enacted moral life intelligible. In other words, the concrete judgments of the natural law apply in virtue of their place in a larger scheme.[46]

In the striking essay "Natural Law as Subversive: The Case of Aquinas," in the process of positioning Aquinas in terms of the political struggles of the thirteenth century, MacIntyre observes that Aquinas's interventions are supported exclusively by appeal to arguments drawn from Christian theology. MacIntyre suggests that insofar as Aquinas was faithful to his conception of natural law, he was at odds with the persecutory activities of the centralized powers of his day but was so not on the basis of his conception of natural law.[47]

Aquinas's conception of natural law plays its part in what MacIntyre identifies as the Christian doctrine of God. That doctrine, that is, the doctrine that God alone exists by necessity, indicates why the sheer contingency by which every enacted story begins requires a doctrine of creation and the possibility of an ending—which means not only was there a beginning but there must also be a doctrine of an ultimate end, which some call the Last Judgment.[48]

MacIntyre elaborates on these claims by suggesting that every human life has the form of an enacted human narrative. That is why every human life must be lived as a story whose truthfulness depends on its being embedded in a larger narrative of which it is but an episode— thus the recognition that there are narratives within narratives. Those narratives ultimately will be located "within that history whose beginning is told in Genesis and whose ending is told in the Apocalypse of John."[49] That seems to mean, therefore, that the necessity that our lives have narrative coherence begs for a theological display, and that MacIntyre, as a philosopher, thinks he can only suggest its form. We might like him to do more, but we should not complain because he has given us more than most contemporary philosophers think possible.

7

Wounded

THE CHURCH AND PASTORAL CARE

Establishing Credentials

I could not help but notice, at a conference meant to attract vocations
to the priesthood, that I was one of the few speakers on the program
who was not ordained.[1] At such a conference I assume it is a good thing
to have priests doing most of the work. But I also have a stake in that
project. As a representative of the laity, I care deeply about the kind of
folk called to the ministry because I have to suffer their inadequacies—
a fate I happily have avoided at the Church of the Holy Family in Chapel
Hill, North Carolina, whose clergy are certainly more adequate than
I am as a layperson.

There is another anomaly about my lay status. I am charged with
the task of giving a theological account of the necessity of pastoral
care as one of the essential practices of the church. It may be the case
that pastoral care is primarily associated with those ordained, but I do
not believe that what makes pastoral care "pastoral" is that it is done
primarily by the ordained.

Pastoral care is the work of the whole church even if in reality our
care of one another currently seems primarily to fall on the clergy. Of

course, most of what the clergy do is the work of the whole church, but that is why some are given particular responsibility to see that such work be done. We, that is the laity, expect the clergy to visit the sick, counsel those seeking to end their marriage, pray with a family whose child has just died, help a gay couple overcome their anger at the church, force an addict to recognize they are an addict, confront a member of the vestry about a racist remark they made, and/or suggest to a member of the church who insists on wearing a Trump baseball hat to Rite One that such a hat is inappropriate in worship. The list could go on; it is infinite.

The challenge facing my attempt to say how I think the clergy ought to care pastorally for those so wounded is not only that I am a layperson but I am not burdened with having a reputation for being pastorally sensitive. I did go to seminary, and I was assigned to a church in which I bore the responsibility for keeping the Methodist Youth Fellowship (MYF) entertained by giving them an infinite series of group experiences. The primary form of group experience turned out to be, at least in New England, taking the kids to bowl duck pins. Under the influence of Barth, I finally told this group of young people that if they were only coming to church under threat from their parents, they should just stay home, and about half of them took me up on the suggestion by ceasing to come to Sunday-night MYF. As we say in Texas, some of their parents were "none too pleased."

All of which is a way to acknowledge that I am not a guy known for insightful work in pastoral theology. For example, I had my decision not to seek ordination confirmed just as I was graduating from seminary. I ran into Gay Noyce in the hall at Yale Divinity School. Gay was a great-souled person who taught pastoral care courses, in addition to running fieldwork, at Yale. Gay asked me what I was planning to do upon graduation. I reported I had been accepted into the Ph.D. program so I was staying on to do a graduate degree. Gay responded by observing that he often tried to convince those intent on pursuing a Ph.D. to think again and consider going into the ministry. He then quickly added, "As far as you are concerned, Stanley, I think you are making the right decision."

Given the direction my work has taken over the years, I suspect many would think Professor Noyce's judgment well-confirmed. Shorthand summaries of what I have been about such as "the first task of the church is not to make the world more just but to make the world the world" do not sound very pastoral. Even worse is my claim that "in the shadows of a dying Christendom the challenge is how to recover a strong theological voice without that voice betraying the appropriate fragility of all speech but particularly speech about God" does not sound like a stance that has much time for taking seriously the wounds of a people in advanced industrial societies who along the way discover their lives are without meaning.[2] My general view is, what did they expect? My advice for those so identified is for them to quit taking themselves so seriously. What they need is to have their narcissism countered by being drawn into the eschatological mission of the church to witness to Christ's cross and resurrection. Doing that I take to be what pastoral care should be about for no other reason than it gives us, as followers of Jesus, good work to do, and what could be more important than that?

Given these judgments, you will not be surprised to learn that I have little sympathy for clergy who think their ministry of pastoral care to be the expression of a more general stance identified as a helping profession. Admittedly those who so understand their ministry may often manifest pious pretentions necessary to justify their self-proclaimed identity as someone who responds to a crisis "pastorally," but I do not think such piety is sufficient to justify describing what they do as a church practice.

There is the problem, moreover, that when the ministry becomes just another form of the helping professions, those who occupy that office discover they have no protection from those they are supposed to help. People think they can ask those who identify as "helpers" to do anything because those committed to be a "helper" do not work for a living. As a result, it does not take long before those in the ministry who identify as "helpers" soon discover they feel like they have been nibbled to death by ducks. A little bite here and a little bite there, and before they know it they have lost an arm. As a result, those who started out wanting to be "of help" often end up violently disliking those whom they are allegedly helping.

Insofar as the ministry is understood as a helping profession it is difficult to avoid an alienation between those who help and those who need help. One of the great gifts of being in the ministry is the permission it gives to be present to people in crisis when they are often at the most vulnerable point in their life. They are often appreciative that you are present during the crisis, but after the crisis is over they prefer that you be kept at a distance. They excommunicate those who have been present during the crisis because they fear those who have seen them when they were so vulnerable. That they do so makes the upbuilding of the community at the very least difficult.

Clearing Some of the Swamp

More needs to be said about the pathologies surrounding pastoral care, but I think it important to step back just a bit to provide what I hope is a perspective on the work of pastoral care that makes such care so important for the upbuilding of the church. I think you have to begin with the basics. To be a human being is to be subject to being wounded in countless ways. In his insightful book *Incarnational Ministry: Being with the Church,* Sam Wells distinguishes being troubled from being hurt, afflicted, and challenged. He does so to suggest how being with those who are afflicted is a particular challenge given that affliction seems to have no end. Yet Wells argues that the Christian understandings of ministry mean we have the obligation to be present to one another, particularly when we are those who are wounded, in a manner that those wounds do not isolate us. We are not called to be perpetually strong. We need to know how to ask for help. Such help, moreover, we believe to be an indication of how God would have the church be a witness to a world that seems to think it does not have the time to care for the wounded.[3]

I assume, therefore, that pastoral care is an essential practice that makes the church the church, but I do not understand why that means that pastoral care and pastoral theology should be understood as a distinct practice and/or discipline. In his informative book *Leading God's People: Wisdom from the Early Church for Today*, Christopher Beeley rightly argues that one of the fundamental pastoral tasks the Fathers thought incumbent on the pastor was to "Strengthen the flocks under you. Encourage them with the apostolic writings; lead them with the Gospels; counsel them with the Psalms."[4] So was the pastoral task understood to be but part of the general project of what it means to build up the church in holiness.

Some worry, however, if the pastoral task is understood as the building up of the church in holiness, then the church cannot be prophetic. That the church cannot be both because it is assumed that there is a fundamental difference between the pastoral and the prophetic tasks of the church.[5] The most charitable interpretation of the dualism between the pastoral and the prophetic is to think that distinction reflects the traditional division between the priestly and prophetic offices that has characterized the ministry of the church. I assume those offices can have quite different expressions and perhaps even be in tension, but that does not mean they are exclusive alternatives. At least they are not exclusive alternatives if you remember they are both necessary for the church to be the church.

For example, for a people to exist who have been given the time to care for the dying in a world that increasingly thinks such care is a waste of time is at once prophetic and pastoral. We dare not forget that care for the dying is one of the essential pastoral tasks Christians enact. Thus my judgment that if in a hundred years Christians are identified as people who do not kill their children or the elderly, we will have done well. Yet what an extraordinary pastoral challenge it is to form and sustain a people who have not let their desire to be compassionate in the face of their neighbors' suffering turn them into killers.

I think all I have just said about the importance of pastoral care is true, but I still do not understand how or why there needed to be something called pastoral care as well as pastoral theology that is distinguished from just plain old theology. Sarah Coakley explores how this division may have occurred by reminding us of David Kelsey's analysis, in his *Beyond Athens and Berlin,* of Schleiermacher's attempt to make theology a professional discipline in the University of Berlin. Coakley observes that this had the effect, an unintended effect, of making theology affectively orientated and antirational.[6]

This has resulted, I fear, in making much of the work done in the name of pastoral care and pastoral theology to be conceived and justified in a manner such that God became an afterthought. Coakley calls attention to the extraordinary influence of Anton Boisen, who founded the CPE movement, whose method of "living documents" she describes as potentially providing a profound learning experience. Yet she also describes the theology that informs that method as "derisory anti-intellectual shavings from the table of university theological discourse."

Of course, pastoral care has always been a characteristic of how Christians have understood their responsibility for one another. But that care has taken diverse forms throughout Christian history. Though I am not happy that "pastoral care" is distinguished from what the church does when it baptizes and communes, I do not mean to deny that Christians have rightly cared for, supported, and sustained one another when they have been beset with illness, betrayals, poverty, and the general slings and arrows that are inevitable given the fact we are fleshly beings. That Christians have so cared for one another, moreover, has a history worth a brief reminder.

Historical Ramblings

As I noted above, although the care Christians give one another is not limited to those who are designated as priests and ministers, it is nonetheless the case that those charged with priestly functions often find they have the responsibility to provide care for those who suffer.

This has been true throughout Christian history as William Clebsch and Charles Jackle's *Pastoral Care in Historical Perspective* as well as G. R. Evans's *A History of Pastoral Care* make clear.[7] If you can write a history of pastoral care, that must surely mean that it exists.

But those histories also help us see that what has been meant by pastoral care has differed across time. For example, Clebsch and Jackle identify at least eight different epochs of Christian pastoral care, each with its own emphases. In the first era of Christian existence, pastoral care was understood to be the sustaining of souls through the vicissitudes of life. The church under persecution meant the pastoral task became the reconciling of troubled persons to God and the church. The political and social establishment of the church meant the goal of pastoral care was now understood as the guidance necessary to have the laity behave according to the norms of what was now assumed to be constitutive of a Christian culture. This pastoral project was supplemented later around a sacramental system designed to heal all maladies. The Reformation and Enlightenment focused on that newly discovered character, namely the individual, who needed help if they were to pass through the pitfalls of a threatening world as the subject of pastoral care.[8]

Clebsch and Jackle are more than ready to acknowledge that these generalizations about how pastoral care was understood across time are just that, namely, generalizations that oversimplify these different epochs. Yet I think their attempt to remind us that pastoral care, a relatively recent description, reflects different understandings of what it means to be wounded is important. In short, any attempt to understand the work done in the name of pastoral care will often draw on what it means to be wounded in this particular time and place. Accordingly, any attempt to develop a theological account of pastoral care will require some presuppositions drawn from the cultures in which the church finds itself. Such an account entails the difficult task of determining what narratives we are living out—narratives that are often unknown to us.

Clebsch and Jackle identify four basic functions that they believe constitute the pastoral ministry of the church: they are healing, sustaining, guiding, and reconciling.[9] Of course, what each of these practices entailed would differ from one time and place to another time and place, but Clebsch and Jackle maintain that some form of each of them has always been present in the church. For example, they observe that in the early Middle Ages catechetical training for the moral life was dependent on the classification of sins with appropriate penalties enumerated in the penitential manuals. That the manuals are now thought of as "ethics" is but an indication that the distinction between pastoral care and moral formation could not be imagined.

I call attention to Clebsch and Jackle's historical account of pastoral care to help us understand why the recent developments in pastoral care and pastoral theology are so significant. They observe that at the heart of pastoral care is an understanding of what it means to be a being that can be hurt as well as how we should respond to being hurt. What it means to be hurt, to be a vulnerable human being, is a correlate of an understanding of human personhood they argue has assumed a particular character in this time called "modern." According to Clebsch and Jackle, the conviction that any limit on our desires is problematic is in deep tension with traditional assumptions. Pastoral care now means helping people become self-fulfilled when it is not clear what that might mean.[10]

That transformation of what is meant by pastoral care Clebsch and Jackle suggest is obvious given the different reasons people now go to seek help from the pastor. They observe that not that long ago people went to their pastor because they felt bad, but today people seek therapy not because they feel bad but because they do not feel good. This has had the effect of putting extraordinary pressure on marriage and the family because often people focus on the family, and in particular their marriage, as the source of their unhappiness.

Clebsch and Jackle point out that there simply is no place in the structure of modern congregation where a serious discussion of the state of one's soul can be examined. That absence reflects the presumption that what we do with our lives is our own business. Some form of counseling now becomes the paradigm of pastoral care. The character of such counseling is not easily identified because there are numerous psychological theories that inform those doing the counseling. As H. Richard Niebuhr observed in his *The Purpose of the Church and Its Ministry,* a book well worth revisiting, the modern conception of human nature that has shaped the church's pastoral care has underwritten a naturalistic anthropology and as a result the religious character of our lives has been lost.[11]

Ramblings in the Present

I think we get some idea of the character of contemporary understandings of pastoral care by attending to MacIntyre's account in *After Virtue* of the main characters who have authority in modernity, that is, the rich aesthete, the manager, and the therapist. Each, in their own way, is an expression of a culture of emotivism that is based on the presumption that insofar as our lives make sense, they do so only by the imposition of our arbitrary willfulness. Such willfulness is required because it is assumed that our lives have no end other than what we can create and impose by the sheer force of our arbitrary desires. As a consequence, it becomes impossible to avoid the reality that all our interactions are unavoidably manipulative. In such a context, the task of the therapist is to "transform neurotic symptoms into directed energy, maladjusted individuals into well-adjusted ones."[12] The therapist must do so, moreover, assuming that there is no normative framework other than respect for their clients' autonomy that can shape their interactions.

To be a moral agent in such a culture entails that we can never be fully in actions because if we are to be free, we must always be able to stand back from our actions as if someone other than ourselves did what was done. Such a perspective is our only way to avoid being determined by particularistic narratives that would constrain our choices. The therapist cannot avoid reflecting these conditions because the therapist cannot assume a narrative that can help us make sense of the moral incoherence of our lives. Thus MacIntyre's claim in *Ethics in the Conflicts of Modernity: An Essay on Desire, Practical Reasoning, and Narrative* that any challenge to these modern habits of thought faces the difficulty of only being able to think about our lives in terms that exclude those concepts needed for any radical critique.[13]

What MacIntyre helps us see is how the eclectic character of the various psychological theories that so often inform pastoral care reflects liberal political theory and practice. That many people in advanced industrial societies suffer from a sense that they are alone because no one—including themselves—understands who they are is the expected result of living in a time when freedom is assumed to be found in having unimpeded choice.

Adrian Pabst observes that such a view of life is the outworking of the basic logic of capitalist economy, which destroys human attachment to, and affections for, relationships and institutions by embedding them in impersonal exchanges. As a result, people are abstracted from concrete human relations because the economy treats everyone as a commodity with a market price. The result is seldom noted because the ideologies that are commensurate with capitalism are grounded in abstractions from any embodiments that constitute our humanity.[14]

Thus my oft-made claim that modernity names the time when people came to believe they should have no story determining their lives except the story they chose when they had no story. In America that story we assume is the story called freedom. That story produces people who think they have been wounded by being born. To so understand the human condition reflects the double-bind insight that what we thought we did in freedom turns out to be but another name for being fated by what can only appear retrospectively as our arbitrary choices.

That story grounds our presumption that we have been mistreated, that we have been victimized, because we discover we cannot acknowledge we have been determined by the story we thought was our choice.

Accordingly, we resent the lives we have forged because somewhere along the line, if we are lucky—and luck is a Stoic category—we are forced to acknowledge we have been wounded by what we thought to be our free decisions. I take it to be one of the fundamental convictions of Christians that we have been given a way to life that frees us from this kind of endemic narcissism that would otherwise possess our lives.

That counseling is now central for how pastoral care is understood, I think is a response to this general unease about our lives. Pastoral care became a necessary course to train clergy to help people, which include themselves, to come to terms with the incoherence of our lives. In the process those seeking therapy might also be able to acknowledge whom they hurt along the way as well as who has hurt them. The language of reconciliation can cover a multitude of sins. I am aware that the training in the psychological disciplines that shape pastoral care may be more substantive than this characterization, but the general worry to avoid being judgmental makes it difficult to articulate a normative commitment other than avoiding being judgmental.

It is not surprising that the theology that shaped the development of pastoral theology was primarily various forms of Protestant liberalism. Liberal theology comes in many shapes and sizes, but in general, to use Barth's characterization, liberal theology was the attempt to talk about God by talking about humanity in a very loud voice. Paul Tillich was the theologian who provided a theological method, that is, the method of correlation that was designed to show how interpretations of central theological concepts could illuminate aspects of human experience.[15] Tillich's "method" had the advantage of employing psychotherapeutic insights as well as other social sciences to illumine the human condition.[16]

But that "advantage" is also the problem if you think, as I do, that such a method risks isolating those who are in need of pastoral care from the church. That some people trained in pastoral care now become freestanding therapists, freestanding in the sense they have no authorization from any ecclesial body, is the inevitable outcome of the development of pastoral care as a separate discipline without theological warrant. Simply because such therapist are ordained does not mean their work is "pastoral."

Perhaps even more troubling is Stephen Pattison's suggestion that the psychological perspective threatens to subordinate the "historical concern of the church for morality and the goals and purpose of human life."[17] As a result Pattison argues that secular caring methods are unconsciously allowed to seep into Christian attempts at pastoral care. In the name of love the Christian care of one another is determined by a utilitarian logic that underwrites a morality that cannot help but result in judgments that make the Christian commitments, commitments such as our unwillingness to keep the promises we make, problematic.

I think it not accidental that the rise of pastoral care and pastoral theology was matched in ethics with the development of situations ethics. Joseph Fletcher's "love is the only norm" seemed to express the fundamental judgment associated with pastoral responses to difficult human relations, particularly having to do with marriage. Fletcher's justification of cases such as Mrs. Bergmeier's "sacrificial adultery" fit the commitment of those doing pastoral counseling to avoid being "moralistic."[18] Those influenced by Fletcher's identification of agape with utilitarianism often failed to recognize that the justification of adultery in the name of love construed in utilitarian logic is the same logic that justified dropping the bombs on Japan.

The account of the development of pastoral care I have just given does not do justice to the complexity of much of the work done under the heading of pastoral care and pastoral theology. I am not apologizing because I think, as Stephen Pattison has argued, that the pastoral care movement, particularly in America, has ignored the theological tradition that makes the care given through the church Christian.[19] It is not at all clear that Christians are called to be mature or well adjusted, but it is surely the case that the care Christians give one another, and particularly the care that is thought to be the province of those who occupy the pastoral office, will and should depend on being an expression of the fundamental convictions that make Christians Christian. We are not without resources for such an endeavor. And one of those resources has the name Karl Barth.

Barth and Pastoral Care

Deborah Hunsinger begins her book *Theology and Pastoral Counseling: A New Interdisciplinary Approach* by observing that pastoral counselors have not been interested in the theology of Karl Barth. She notes, however, that Barth returned the compliment by paying little attention to the discipline of pastoral counseling and care.[20] It is important, however, not to forget the significant fact that Barth was a pastor in Geneva and Safenweil. That engagement clearly left a lifetime mark on him. In one of his last interviews, which was primarily about his love of Mozart, Barth responded to a question about why he did not continue to be a pastor by observing: "My whole theology, you see, is fundamentally a theology for pastors. It grew out of my own situation when I had to teach and preach and counsel a little. And I found that what I had learned in the university was of little help in this. So I had to make a fresh start and I tried to do this."[21]

Barth began his reflections on the care that the church is to provide by observing that the church had recently seemed to reawaken to its political and social responsibilities. It thus has the task to face ever anew the questions and challenges raised by the modern developments in psychology and education. According to Barth, the church will be asked, "What is pastoral care?" and "What is Christian education?," which means the church should not and cannot attempt to escape the necessity of remembering the challenges raised by its presence in "a world engulfed in a sea of misery." Such a world is waiting—not for the church but—to become church itself. It is waiting to hear because God has spoken.[22]

Hunsinger calls attention to Barth's exploration of the place of pastoral care in terms of the relationship between the forgiveness of sin and healing. Barth observes that, in Mark's account of Jesus's healing of the paralytic, Jesus does not first say, "You are healed," but rather "Your sins are forgiven." The scribes who were present challenged Jesus for acting as if he has the authority to forgive sins. Jesus seems to side with them, acknowledging that only the Son of Man has such authority. It is by such authority, moreover, that Jesus tells the young man to stand up, take up his mat, and go home. Drawing on Barth's reflections of this healing miracle, Hunsinger observes that for Barth the forgiveness of sins is clearly differentiated from healing yet they both occur in a single event. For Barth, therefore, healing is placed in the larger context of a theological claim about Jesus's identity (66).

In 1934 Barth delivered lectures in France that became a small book entitled *God in Action,* which can be read as a mini *Dogmatics.* It is therefore not surprising that in the first lecture Barth develops his account of revelation and why it is the necessary starting point for all theology. He argues, in typical Barthian fashion, that any knowledge of God we may have is and has been brought about by the initiative of a sovereign God.[23] For Barth God's, reconciliation with us is not a truth that revelation makes known but reconciliation is the truth of God Himself. Because revelation is God Himself, the church must contend against all forms of knowledge that would subordinate theological claims to other discourses. When the church thinks it must translate the gospel into idioms that are not Christologically disciplined, the result is the transformation of theology into ideology. In the process the church is secularized.[24]

Accordingly, what must be called into question, Barth argues, is the modern presumption, a presumption given philosophical status by Descartes, that people no longer worry if God exists. Now we worry what meaning our existence may have. We worry if we exist because we have no sense that we are dependent creatures.[25] We no longer recognize that our very existence is a gift that requires ongoing training that comes by being made a disciple of Christ. The name of that community which makes discipleship possible is called "church."

Pastoral care is not, therefore, some specialized arena that is distinguished from the everyday work of the church. But if the church is to provide the care for one another that is an expression of our being a people whose sins are forgiven, Barth identifies two mistakes that the church must avoid. The first mistake is when the church thinks it is divine revelation institutionalized and as a result cannot acknowledge its essential humanity. Thus Barth's oft-made contention that the church reflects the glory of God but a reflection is not a possession. But it is equally and perhaps even more destructive when, as is often the case in Protestantism, the church is considered just another voluntary association. Both these mistakes place too much trust in our insights and trust God too little. For the church faithfully to exist means it must be sustained by the courage that comes from the work of the Holy Spirit. A church so constituted calls into question all false courage that is based on large numbers, moral qualities, programs of action, or being admired by those without.[26]

That Barth is such a fruitful resource for helping us know how to provide pastoral care for one another is not because what he has to say about pastoral care is so thoughtful. Barth is helpful not for what he says but for what he does not say. He does not say as a community the church is primarily about a compassionate response to our mainly self-inflicted wounds. For Barth pastoral care is an expression of the Christological center of the church's faith that makes possible the care of Christian and non-Christian alike who have been wounded. Those wounds help Barth locate our lives in an ongoing narrative that reflects God's glory in the world. At the very least that glory is manifest in the existence of a people who have been storied by a gracious God.

Some may worry that the church is too far gone to be such a presence, but in fact the church already has the resources to reclaim the pastoral office as an expression of the work of the Holy Spirit. If you doubt that, I ask you to turn to the section of the Book of Common Prayer identified as the "Pastoral Offices." There we have prayers such as "For the Sanctification of Illness" in which we pray, "Sanctify,

O Lord, the sickness of your servant N., that the sense of her weakness may add strength to her faith and seriousness to her repentance; and grant that she may live with you in everlasting life; through Jesus Christ our Lord. Amen."

I should like to think that the humanity of such a prayer Barth would think matched his extraordinary love of all things human. For Barth nothing human is foreign to what it means to be Christian.[27] What could be more human, to be at home in the world, than the worship of a God whose Son is to be found in Mary's belly? A church determined by such a narrative has the capacity to identify and refuse to serve the idols of this world. That Christians refuse such idols will sometimes result in persecution because the idols of the world cannot stand to be ignored. Because Christians do not try to be more than human, they are more humanistic than the humanist just to the extent that we have learned to confess that we are not our own creator.[28]

Pastoral care is an office to be filled not only by the ordained, but there is no question that those set aside to preside at the Eucharist have a particular responsibility for the wounded. We worship a wounded savior. We follow as a people also wounded. Such a people cannot help but care for one another in a manner that imitates God's care for our wounds. They must be, therefore, persons who have learned to be in the presence of suffering without resorting to simplistic explanations. When all is said and done, pastoral care requires those who are to be agents of care to be people of deep humanity.

The challenge is how do you train someone to be a human being? Often people of judgment seem to come from nowhere, and we are mystified in their presence. Yet such people have to exist if we are to be the church that offers one another the care that binds the wounds of death. Whether there is a discipline of pastoral care or pastoral theology I suspect matters little. What matters is that we are wounded people caring for one another in the name of that wound called "the Christ."

You may well be wondering why, given the rather dour character of this chapter, why anyone would want to go into the priesthood. But I hope some of you will draw another conclusion. I hope you will see the difference that Jesus makes for our care of one another and how that difference makes a life of joy possible. If at least some of what I have said is right, then I cannot imagine a more satisfying vocation than that of a priest. At the very least, to be a priest is to be given good work to do. What more could one want than to have your life so consumed?

8

The Church in Asia

A BARTHIAN MEDITATION

Without Authority

I come to you as one without authority.[1] At least I am without the kind of authority that comes from knowing enough to say something useful to those who know more than you do. I know so little about the challenges the churches of Asia face that I am sure I do not even know what I do not know. Most of you have more useful theological observations to make about the churches you serve than I do. So you might well ask, "Why is Hauerwas here?" I have no ready answer other than you wanted to hear a Texas accent. It may be that you also want someone to tell you why it seems Americans have gone crazy, and you assumed someone from Texas might have something to say about that. Texans probably do have something distinctive to say about our current national politics because we have long endured weird people in public office, but that is a subject for another time.

I have been told, however, that one of the reasons I have been asked to speak to you is that in debates in your countries concerning the role Christians should play in politics I am appealed to as an authority by all sides.[2] I had not realized I had such a role in Asia, where it seems

I am more favorably received and understood than I am in the West. I cannot help but think I may be more positively read in Asia than in the West because Asian Christianity has the advantage of never having been socially, politically, or economically established. So what I have had to say about the recovery of the Christian witness to God, a God it seems who does not necessarily vote democratic, may not seem as radical or crazy to you as it does to many Americans.

Christianity in the West is dying of its "success." Christians have managed to make what it means to be a Christian a matter of believing this or that. People think they have a "personal relationship with God" which they go to church to express. It simply is unthinkable to think that salvation is an ecclesial matter. The Catholic view that without the church there is no salvation strikes most Americans as antidemocratic. It is, of course, antidemocratic, but that does not make it any less true. But then "true" is not a word many Christians in America associate with being Christian.

That I may have said things that are useful to you means I have much to learn from you. What you may have found useful or even true may involve matters I did not recognize as all that important. I think that such a process is not unusual because as Christians we cannot help but say more than we know because we do not make Christianity up, but rather we receive the gospel. We receive, moreover, more than we can know.

For example, some years ago I was asked to write a foreword to the Japanese translation of *Resident Aliens*. I was more than happy to do what I was asked to do, but I expressed surprise that that book was relevant to the Japanese church. Will Willimon and I thought the audience for the book was pastors who had long made peace with the accommodated churches of American Protestantism. We were trying to help Christians in America to recover what an extraordinary thing it is that God showed up in the person of a first-century Jew. What little I had learned about Christianity in Japan made me think if there was any people who did not need this book, it was the Japanese. I had assumed that if you are a Christian in Japan, you are a "resident alien," or at least I thought that to be the case because Christians in Japan told me that when they became Christian they were no longer thought to be Japanese.

It was explained to me, however, that it was not being a Christian qua Christian that those who had translated the book thought to be important for Japanese Christians. What they thought particularly important for the church of Japan was the emphasis in the book on the social character of the salvation wrought in Christ. They explained that the early Protestant missionaries to Japan had an individualistic understanding of salvation. As a result, the significance of the church as the embodiment of salvation was lost. So the stress in *Resident Aliens* on God's care of us through the church was a significant emphasis for Japanese Christians.

The stress on the corporate character of what the Presiding Bishop of the Episcopal Church of America, Bishop Michael Curry, calls the "Jesus movement" came home to me in Japan. I had been asked to preach at a church somewhere in Tokyo. I am a lectionary preacher, and the text assigned for the day I was to preach was Ephesians 2:11–21. That happens to be one of my favorite passages from Scripture because I think it is one of the central texts for how we should understand the peace of God. By breaking down of the walls between Jews and Gentiles, a "new humanity" is created that just is God's peace. Peace so understood is not some ideal never to be realized; it is a peace you can see and touch. As I delivered the sermon I could not help but wonder how such a text is received in Japan, where there are few actual Jews. That new reality, the household of God, that is built on the foundation of the apostles and prophets, whose cornerstone is Christ himself, surely must look different in Japan than it did in the ancient Near East. Such a difference is a reminder that the form Christianity takes in different and diverse cultures will be distinctive. Yet that distinctiveness must not prevent Christians from recognizing one another as Christian brothers and sisters in Christ, though they may look very different.

This last observation may be the reason I have been asked to address you. My work as a theologian has stressed the importance for Christians in the West to recover the witness to Christ's Lordship in a manner that makes clear that all that is is storied by that grand story called Trinity. Yet the assumed familiarity with Christianity by many in the United States almost makes it impossible for those in societies like America to hear the radical character of the gospel. I have tried to express what I take to be the challenge before the socially established churches of the West with this sentence: "In the shadows of a dying Christendom the challenge is how to recover a strong theological voice without that voice betraying the fragility of all speech—but particularly speech about God." I have argued that the recovery of such a voice will require Christians to recognize that we are no longer in control of the social and political orders that were created to make what it means to be Christian and American (or European) an identification without difference. That emphasis has earned me the designation of being a sectarian, fideistic tribalist.

Of course, the disestablishment of Christianity in Western industrialized countries is not yet complete.[3] The very presumption that America is to be made great again is for many a slogan meant to recover something like a (white) Christian America. That America, that is, the Christian America, probably never existed does not prevent many Christians in America from identifying what they assume are democratic regimes with Christianity as a given. The very description of "West" is an indication of the continuing power of a Christendom mentality given the assumption that the West is Christian. Of course, it is never quite clear where the West begins and/or ends. It has always been a curiosity for me how Plato and the Greeks in general became representatives of the West, that is, Greece is the home of Western philosophy. That seems so odd because Greece is clearly East. At least Greece is East depending on where one is standing to make the West the West and the East the East.

But if the West is becoming increasingly free of Christian hegemony, it seems to be the case that the churches of the East may be in the process of finding ways to institutionalize the faith. Could it be that we are in danger of passing one another in the night? I know, or at least think I know, given the difficulty of being Christians in the societies from which you come, the idea that you may be in the business of a Christendom project may seem absurd. Yet as Bruce Kaye observes in his fine book *The Rise and Fall of English Christendom: Theocracy, Christology, Order and Power,* the first Christians had to face the passing of generations, which meant they had to find a way to hand their faith on to the next generation: "Thus began a process of tradition and that in time inevitably meant institutions of one kind or another."[4] If Kaye is right, it seems Christendom is built into the DNA of Christianity.

Though I am identified as an anti-Christendom theologian, I have always assumed that there can be no Christianity without the production of the kind of material innovations Kaye's quote suggests are intrinsic to Christian practice. Moreover, the kind of institutions created to perform that task will rightly often mimic, if not take on, forms that are decidedly local. Thus Kaye's suggestion that Bede's great achievement was to present in his history the idea that the English people would constitute a form of political life through monarchy that would make the church integral to their being a Christian nation.[5] Kaye's observation about the form English Christendom took is a nice example of the claim made above that Christianity will look quite different from one context to another.

Kaye notes, however, that this emphasis on the local character of Christian formations cannot help but create tensions within Christianity itself. Drawing on Peter Brown's great work *Western Christendom,* Kaye describes the conundrum this creates by asking, if Christianity is a universal religion, which it surely is, why does Christianity not have a universal organizational structure?[6] Thus the ecclesiological question of what kind of connectedness between Christian assemblies is possible that can deal with the diversity of practices and forms and still claim to be the same religion.[7]

One response to this conundrum is the attempt to force a unity on the church by the authority of government and/or the law. This can be called the "Christendom strategy," which Kaye describes as any community located within some discernible framework or polity that sees itself as Christian, making possible a coalescence of power that coercively ensures a common way of life.[8] The forms of coercion to ensure a Christendom strategy can be quite subtle as well as overtly violent. That Christendom can and has taken many different forms is perhaps nowhere better exemplified than in Mennonite farm culture, which is establishment Christianity with no means of recognizing itself as such.

If I understand rightly where you are as the church in Asia, Christendom is not a profound temptation because there is no possibility you can enact a Christendom strategy. I hesitate to use a phrase such as "the church in Asia" because such a description can hide the great differences between the churches in, for example, Korea and the churches in China. Indeed, such a phrase can erase the difference between the house and megachurches in China. I use the phrase, however, because I think in general it is true that the church in Asia is in little danger of being tempted to institutionalize yourself through the agency of government or even through what appear to us to be noncoercive forms of social life such as the establishment of educational institutions. Yet it must surely be the case that it is difficult to resist trying to imagine ways the church can be institutionalized in your quite different cultures that can ensure the church will continue to the next generation. Why should you not try to make the gospel available as a given because the very fact you exist seems like a miracle?

Just as one of the extraordinary facts of recent times is the continuing faith of African Americans in the God they received in slavery. In like manner, it is remarkable that Asian Christians did not let the bad behavior of missionaries stop them from becoming Christians. The missionaries came from Christendom churches, but they discovered through witness to the gospel that Christianity could thrive as a free church. Habits are hard to break, which makes me worry whether it is possible for the church in Asia to avoid the mistakes of those from whom they received the gospel, that is, those who represented a Christianity that could not be separated from its nationalistic home.

I do not want to be misunderstood. Like many, I have been influenced by revisionist accounts of mission that rightly suggest that those called to mission often were changed by the God they discovered in those to whom they had come to bear witness. I think Dana Robert gets the matter right when she observes that the fascinating issue raised by mission history is not why the Christian message was rejected by people of diverse cultures, but why it was so widely accepted.[9] I think she is also right that the retreat of Christianity in the face of secular criticism and anticolonialism turns out not to be the end of a world Christianity, but the "death rattle of European Christianity," which includes the churches of America.[10]

Robert is not trying to justify the cultural imperialism that was often confused with what was taken to be a witness to the gospel. She rightly notes that many Western missionaries, particularly those who were highly educated, because of their theological convictions, did turn out to be hegemonic fanatics. Robert observes that even acts such as teaching people to read or to dig wells to secure clean water can be seen as an assault on indigenous culture. Though missionaries seldom carried guns, they had the backing of Western economics and politics that pressured people to change their cultures.[11] The challenge, of course, is that some cultures or aspects of culture are surely rightly to be changed by the gospel—think, for example, what it would mean if the church tried to find a way not to be the American church but instead found itself to be the church that happens to exist in America. If the latter church existed, Christians might discover they have more to say about race than they thought.

Peter Leithart, currently one of the most insightful theologians in America, in his recent book *The End of Protestantism: Pursuing Unity in a Fragmented Church*, observes that American Protestant denominationalism has been most clearly defined by giving enthusiastic support to virtually every American war.[12] Such a church may appear quite tolerant as well as tolerated at least as long as the difference from other religious communities does not challenge the more important national consensus. What such churches have in common, however, is not a catholic commitment to unity based on the cross but rather the American general sense that you should "live and let live." Christianity was not legally established in America, but it did not need legal establishment because it was the socially established religion of America through the centuries of American life.[13]

The place of immigrants in American society is revealing in this respect. Leithart observes that immigrants are at once accepted yet distrusted by Protestant Americans. This strange contradictory position is the result of American expectations that immigrants should at once be grateful to be in America yet they continue to have strong ties and loyalties to their home country. The result is the children of emigrants lose their cultural identity as soon as possible by becoming Americans. The only difficulty with those strategies by those who have come to America is they will never be trusted to be good Americans.[14]

Leithart thinks, however, as I have suggested, that the Protestant establishment is collapsing and as a result the American civil religion that depended on that establishment is undergoing erosion. Leithart hopes that such a development will open up the possibility of what he calls a "Reformational Catholicism" that can preserve the theological emphases of the Reformation while recovering the catholic character of the church. The latter Leithart thinks is best pursued at the local level, which he thinks will require each Protestant church restoring the weekly celebration of the Lord's supper. Leithart does not pretend that this will make life easier, but, as he says: "When Jesus comes to dinner every week, things happen. Strange things. The church may split. All hell may break loose, and the pastor and other leaders have to pick up the pieces and try to reassemble them."[15] But at least Leithart believes such an unleashing of the Spirit may put us on the way to being a free church.

You may now be wondering where I am going with these reflections. I am supposed to be addressing the challenges the church faces in Asia, but I have shifted the subject to what I know, that is, Protestantism in America. But I think this brief look at the church in America is not without relevance to the church in Asia. For the challenge before you is how to sustain the difference locality makes, that is, what it means to be the Korean, Japanese, Chinese, and other churches in Asia, while remaining in unity with one another. A unity that at the very least is to be found in the Christian unwillingness to kill one another in the name of being Korean, Japanese, or Chinese.

For it must surely be the case that one of the central challenges for Christians in Asia is how to negotiate the rising nationalism that the different countries of the region seem to be developing. The wounds of the past, moreover, remain. Those wounds will not be healed by advising, "just get over it." No, those wounds demand common projects by Christians in the hope we will discover friends we did not know we had through worship and common projects. To be so united in the Spirit is at once the great challenge as well as the great opportunity before the churches of Asia. The refusal to kill turns out to be a great fundamental for the common story Christians share.

Such unity requires a robust theological understanding of the reality of God's kingdom, which I believe can be found in the work of Karl Barth, an odd observation, but one I think defensible by attending to Chloe Starr's book on Chinese theology.

Karl Barth's "Honest Ignorance"

In her book *Chinese Theology: Text and Context,* Professor Chloe Starr has a fascinating chapter on two very different and antagonistic Chinese religious figures—Ding Guangxun and Wang Mingdao.[16] These men were contemporaries who confronted many of the same challenges, but they represent, at least in Starr's account, quite different ways for the church to be the church given the fast-paced changes that modern Asia and in particular China have had and are continuing to experience.[17]

Professor Starr nicely makes evident the difference between these extraordinary men by beginning her chapter on Ding Guangxun and Wang Mingdao with a quote from each of these men that makes their antagonism clear. In 1954 Ding Guangxun wrote asking the question, "Must the church follow a path opposed to our nation?" He intensifies that question, asking further, "Can the church only glorify God by placing itself in opposition to the nation and its people?" He answers with a resounding, "absolutely not."[18] That "absolutely not" is an affirmation of Ding's role as one of the chief apologists for the Three-Self Movement.[19] His theological perspective can be characterized as Reformed but with a Kuyperian direction.

Wang Mingdao, who was from the beginning the great enemy of the Three-Self Movement, was quite critical of Ding. Wang not only opposes Ding, but he is clearly a very different person than Ding. He was, I think, a person who might be characterized in general as "difficult." He was unrelenting in opposing the attempt of the state to control the church, but he was also a forceful critic of internal issues about the character of the church itself.[20] In both areas he proved to be a person of great strength, but one cannot help but feel he had a combative personality.

He was arrested in 1956 only to spend the next twenty years in prison. In 1954, however, prior to his imprisonment, Wang passed judgment on Ding and the Three-Self Movement. Accordingly, Starr quotes Wang's judgment that applied immediately to Ding: "It is lamentable that many Christian leaders use the principle of obedience to man's rules and submission to man's authority to cover up their cowardice and failure . . . This results in the faith of the church and the ministry being subordinated to the rule of men and man's authority. The truth becomes obscured, the Bible misinterpreted, the foundations of the church undermined and the flock scattered. How can such Christian leaders then escape the wrath of God?"[21]

You could not hope to have a more stark contrast. The temptation, particularly for those of us schooled on claims concerning the freedom of the church, is to side with Wang Mingdao. Yet Starr provides a quite positive account, perhaps too positive, of both men. Indeed, she notes in Ding's early writings that he was quite close to Wang Mingdao's evangelical commitments as well as the emphasis on the importance of creedal orthodoxy. Though they may have shared some theological presumptions, they were destined to come into conflict in 1955. That conflict was perhaps due to each man's personality and temperament, but it remains the case that their understanding of the relation of the church to the world was at the center of their dispute.

Both were committed to finding a way to establish the church in Chinese society. Ding, for example, was deeply committed to the development of educational institutions. He had gotten some of his education in Canada and had become for a time the missionary secretary to the Canadian Student Christian Movement. Starr, moreover, reports that throughout his ministry, including his support for the government's Three-Self Movement, Ding combined a genuine respect for others with a desire that they come to know Christ.[22] An Episcopalian, Ding had a high Christology with a strong stress on Jesus's humanity. The emphasis on Jesus, very God and very man, was the basis of Ding's ecclesial convictions that there is a strong continuity between Christ and the church. In some ways Ding can be styled as the Bede of China, at least he could be so interpreted if Bruce Kaye is right to suggest that Bede's great imaginative achievement was to present in his *History* the idea of a political life for the English people that was at once a nation and a church.[23]

Wang Mingdao thought Ding's support of Three-Self Movement was a betrayal of the church. Appeals to Romans 13 were not persuasive. Wang's harsh criticisms often seem justified given Ding's rhetoric from time to time in favor of the government's control of the church. For example, in an article as early as 1953 Ding said, "Under the protection of the People's Government, we have been able to shatter the shackles of imperialism and truly become a church." He, moreover, sees that development as finally a break from the missionary hegemony from which the Chinese church has suffered through the missionary effort. According to Ding, for more than one hundred years the church in China had been manipulated by the corrupt and imperialistic Western church. As a result, the Chinese church did not know what it really believed, hoped for, or loved. The rise of Three-Self Church was for him the beginning necessary to heal the wound he thought Western missionaries had inflicted on Christianity in China.[24]

Central to Ding's position was the conviction that there can be no separation of "church people" from "world people." Theology cannot be a discipline only for self-identified Christians because the church and the world overlap. He, therefore, maintained that to work against the people's liberation movement was ethically indefensible on Christian grounds. Ding and Wang Mingdao seemed destined to reproduce some the classic debates of the Reformation and, perhaps even more significant, the struggle of the church against Hitler.

It is not surprising, therefore, that Starr concludes her chapter on Ding Guangxun with what she calls "A Barthian Meditation." In her meditation she reprises the controversy occasioned by Barth's strong condemnation of the Nazis and later his refusal to condemn Communism in equally strong terms. In particular Starr draws attention to Barth's Letter to Christians in East Germany entitled "How to Serve God in a Marxist Land." In that letter Barth argued that there is no simple answer one can give for those who must live under the rule of Communists. To give any advice, Barth observes, would require one to have lived with the Christians of East Germany as they experienced the growing pressure of the Communist regime. To negotiate such regimes one would need to try out personally the various possibilities of resisting Communism in order to discover some wisdom, which, because of a deficiency of knowledge of the facts, situations, and persons, always threatens to become irrelevant idealism.[25] It is better, therefore, for Christians from outside Eastern Europe to express an "honest ignorance" when confronted by regimes like the Communist Party of East Germany.

By "honest ignorance" Barth means that Christians who live outside Communist Eastern Europe should have the humility to acknowledge they lack the necessary standing to know how to respond to the developing governments in Eastern Europe. Barth's "honest ignorance" is an expression of his disavowal of Christendom. He does not mean that there are not things Christians can do to make life better in Eastern Europe, but that is always to be determined along the way. For Barth, however, there is no substitute for Christians in their different circumstances sharing what they have learned about how to live in the face of an adversary who would deny their existence.

Starr rightly notes, therefore, that Barth's avowal of "honest ignorance" did not stop him from condemning the "spirit, and the words, the methods and the practices" of the East German government as well as the policies of the West toward the East. For Barth all regimes are potential "prowling adversaries" which must be resisted. Such resistance is possible because the God we worship is sovereign over unbeliever as well as the believer. Starr points out that such a stance acknowledges the authority of the state though the state can take a number of different forms. For Barth there is no "such thing as a perfect political system"; there are only better and worse systems.[26] The ability to distinguish the better from the worse begins with the question of whether the church is free to be the church.[27] Thus Barth's recognition that the evil of the Nazi regimes was evident just to the extent Christians were prohibited from preaching to Jews.

Starr's appeal to Barth's "honest ignorance" is an insightful suggestion, but that stance of humility cannot stand apart from Barth's fundamental theological commitments. Barth urges Christians not to favor any one kind of political regime because it is the Kingdom of God itself that shapes the church's politics. The Christian community knows that the pattern of God's order is to be found in the Kingdom of God. The grace of God and the Kingdom of God, the source and end of all Christian teaching, for Barth bears a name, Jesus Christ. The kingdom of God makes possible the Christian political witness to always be present so that the world may know that there is an alternative to the violence that characterizes the relations between peoples and nations.

Barth's "honest ignorance" is the stance of those who worship the One alone who makes possible a people who do not seek to dominate their world. They have no illusion that they are in control of their destiny. It is not necessary, therefore, for Barth to think he would have to choose between Ding and Wang Mingdao, though one cannot help but think that Barth would have worried that Ding was sailing too close to the shore of accommodation to worldly powers.

More important than whose side Barth may have been on is the ecclesial implications of Barth's position. Barth was anything but a Catholic, but if as Bruce Kaye maintains catholicity is understood as the practice of mutual interaction between churches that makes them aware of wider dimensions of the Christian faith than local experience can provide, then Barth can be understood to be a representative of the catholic character of the church.[28] Such an understanding of catholicity, Kaye argues, includes a number of Christian virtues such as patience, mutual respect, and humility. Those are the virtues that are often implicit in Barth as he sought to help Christians to avoid homogenization by learning to respect their differences. In the process Christians may exhibit a politics that can provide fruitful analogies for the politics of the world.

How to Go On

What does this mean for the church in Asia as well as the declining Western church? The suggestion I am about to make may seem to be more a whimper than a bang, but I think it follows from Barth's recommendation of honest ignorance. To live with something like an "honest ignorance" requires the virtues of patience and humility particularly by those from the most impatient cultures such as America. What it means to be a Christian in America or Europe is rightly not the same as what it means to be a Christian in Japan, China, Korea, and/or Hong Kong. The rise of house churches in China strikes me as one of those creative movements, perhaps as creative as monasticism itself, that gospel patience makes possible. I think it is interesting that the early church was basically a house church movement.

I do, however, have a recommendation for the churches in Asia drawn from Barth's theology that some may find surprising. I began this talk with a reference to the necessity for Christians to create institutions that make possible the passing on of the faith. Few tasks are more important for Christian existence today. The churches of Asia must build institutions for sustaining the church's mission through time. Bruce Kaye suggests that he thinks of institutions as the "attempts over time to sustain continuity over time of patterns of relationships between people and of things for a given purpose on the basis of the underlying values of human conduct."[29] The trick is how to develop such institutions without the church becoming at home in the world Christians assume they have created to make them safe. The result of this kind of institution building is that it makes it difficult for Christians to remember what makes them Christians.[30]

Of course what makes Christians Christian is not always self-evident, which means it does not always make sense to try to distinguish Christians from non-Christians. But in a world in which we now exist we should expect that difference to be a reality. The question is what such a difference might look like in the East. As one who just recommended a stance of honest ignorance, it would seem I should keep silent, but I cannot resist suggesting what I take to be the Christian difference in the world as we know it. My recommendation is very simple. I believe that in the future Christians will be witnesses to the gospel to the extent they have learned the basic virtues that make life not only possible but beautiful. In other words, the churches of Asia, as I suspect the church anywhere, must primarily focus on the formation of people who possess the basic virtues that are necessary to live peaceably in a war-torn world.

"To live peaceably in a war-torn world" does not mean that Christians avoid social engagements that may involve conflict. I have recently become aware that I have become the subject of much debate in Hong Kong concerning the place of Christians in the Umbrella Movement. Some interpret my emphasis on the first task of the church to be the church to suggest that Christians should not be involved with the Occupy Central Movement. Given my lack of knowledge concerning what that movement is about, it would be foolish for me to pontificate about how Christians should support or not support that movement, but I can say in principle there is nothing about my understanding of the church that would prevent Christians from participating in such movements. Yet I cannot deny my politics is a politics for the long haul because I believe that the most enduring political developments that seek justice refuse coercive methods in the hope of providing a more lasting peace.[31]

Michael Ignatieff has recently put forward a proposal for how to approach the moral challenges associated with globalization in his book *The Ordinary Virtues: Moral Order in a Divided World*. His book is a report about his participation in the Carnegie Centennial Project to travel the globe for three years to try to answer the question of whether or not globalization is drawing the world together, or are we ever more likely to simply deny some people as not human. They were also to try to find if, beneath the differences, globalization has revealed as well as enhanced whether there are virtues, principles, and rules of conduct that the peoples of the world are beginning to share.[32]

Ignatieff discovered that religion still counts in the lives of millions as consolation, inspiration, and guide, but that secular patterns of belief are making increasing claims on people across the globe. Those secular claims they primarily identified as the use of rights as the language that sustains the ethics of globalization. The language of rights seems to have the most legitimate claim for being a global language particularly because it was picked up by colonial peoples to legitimate their struggles to wrest from Europeans their national independence. Rights claims, moreover, are the expression of the autonomy and self-determination of each person, making any appreciation of the fundamental sociality of our lives difficult.[33]

Ignatieff reports, however, that the somewhat surprising discovery they made as they visited many different contexts was that the human rights discourse turned out to be language used primarily by elites—that is, the educated, middle- or upper-class intellectuals, teachers, students, and many others. The poor may have recourse to rights when they suffer from government coercion, but for the poor, rights language does not express their sense of community. In contrast they found that ordinary virtues such as trust, tolerance, forgiveness, reconciliation, and resilience emerged as the virtues that made peace possible between people who otherwise share nothing in common. Such virtues Ignatieff describes as ordinary because they are anchored in the everyday.

He concludes, therefore, that a global ethic applicable to all people is unimaginable and irrelevant. This is not because ordinary people are unreflective. They often are quite deeply concerned about the injustice in the world, but their moral reflection does not turn on universals as philosophers in the Kantian tradition seem to assume. Rather, for such folk their ethical commitments turn on whether what they are considering entails what is true for them and their community. Ignatieff concludes, therefore, that "secular narratives—the inevitability of technical progress, the spread of democracy, the triumph of liberalism—that provided an illusion of control for the elites mean little to the poor and dispossessed."[34]

Ignatieff writes as a secular person, but his position is one that we Christians can deeply respect. That is to put the matter too weakly. The churches of Asia are confronted by large boulders of despair. The churches of China, Korea, and Japan are centuries old, but in many ways they are still in their early days. God knows we hope that the churches of Asia will be used by the Holy Spirit to vivify the church.

That we must trust in the Holy Spirit is crucial because these churches will be tempted to secure their existence by means that are antithetical to the gospel. But ordinary virtues are already present, ready to shape and reshape our lives that so that we might be patient witnesses to Jesus, who is God's very patience.

9

Race

Beginning with a Beginning

I began teaching at Augustana College in Rock Island, Illinois, in 1968. My first published article was in the Augustana student newspaper. It was entitled "An Ethical Appraisal of Black Power." I do not remember what possessed me to write the paper, but the style of the paper betrays the arrogance of a young man who thought he knew more than he did. The writing, moreover, is embarrassingly bad. From time to time I have been asked for a copy of the paper, but I had somehow lost it in the "mist of history." I do not remember who, but someone found the damn thing and returned it to me. In preparation for writing this chapter I reread it and thought it an interesting historical document I might use to introduce this essay.

So I am going to begin by reproducing the paper "An Ethical Appraisal of Black Power" because I think both positively and negatively it is a marker indicating where I (we) have been, where I (we) still may be, and how I now think I (we) need to think about race.[1] For as I hope to show, fifty years ago in my attempt to defend Black Power there were present issues that continue to be important for our current thinking about race.

Yet I need to be candid; one of the reasons I begin with "An Ethical Appraisal of Black Power" is to respond to the criticism that I have not addressed the problem of race in my work. James Logan charges that "Hauerwas refuses to risk writing constructively about the problem of racism in society at large, or to face squarely and publicly the issue of racism in the White churches as a distortion in the grammar of the Christian faith, is an example of the all-too-familiar silent narrative of collusion prevalent among Euro-American theologians and ethicists."[2] I have high regard for Logan and his work, and I take seriously his charge.

I do not think, however, that I have completely failed to address the issue of race.[3] I have always regarded race as the central challenge we face if America is to have a moral future. To be sure, I have worried that the dramatic character of the race question has meant that questions of class do not receive their due attention. As someone who comes from a working-class background, I continue to think race and class cannot be separated morally. But it is true that I have not written extensively about race. The issue, however, is not whether I or anyone else has written about race but rather how the profound racism that has shaped our lives should shape our most fundamental theological convictions. A paper or a book may not mention race, but it may nonetheless be significant for how we negotiate a world in which racism is deep.

Jonathan Tran has written a very interesting article that argues as a white theologian I have rightly been primarily silent "in the face of the normalizing powers of academic prolixity on issues of race."[4] I hope he is right, but the truth of the matter is I have not been sure how I should write about race as a white person who has enjoyed a privileged place in that world called America and in particular the university. "An Ethical Appraisal of Black Power" I think is a good example of that difficulty because it reeks of the presumption that race is a problem that African Americans need to negotiate so they can join "our" social world. That said, however, I offer the paper—warts and all—as an introduction to where we were, or at least where I was, in the hope we may better understand where we are now on the question of race. So here it is:

"An Ethical Appraisal of Black Power"

The phrase "Black Power" and what it represents has come as a severe shock to many Christians who liked to think of themselves as liberal on the question of race. They feel as if the starved dog they tried to feed has suddenly bitten the hand of the benefactor. Moreover, it has made sentiments such as "All men are loved by God and should therefore be brothers" seem rather shallow, platitudinous, and logically doubtful.

Cherished strategies such as integration that were thought to be the only rational possibility for people who adhered to principles of equality and justice are now declared to be morally perverse. Instead of integration, the liberal seems to confront proposals that can only appear as reverse segregation. Thus the white Christian liberal reaction to Black Power has been mainly one of some resentment and almost complete bewilderment. It has not only challenged their ethical stance, but suddenly all the avenues which relieve the guilt of being white have been cut off by the very people with whom the liberal wished to identify.

As a result, the response to the Black Power movement from Christians has been almost completely negative as it is seen as the denial of the attempt to bring reconciliation between people; or it is totally embraced by some white people because they seem to assume that anything done by an African American today must be accepted simply on the grounds they are African American. In order to avoid these alternatives, I should like to try to evaluate in a discriminating way the ethical significance of the Black Power movement and in the process perhaps help clarify what place the white liberal might have in relationship to it.

The first difficulty one encounters in the attempt to do this is the ambiguity of the phrase "Black Power." It is apparent that many of the proponents of Black Power often understand the phrase in radically different ways. It would be impossible to try to analyze here all the emotive and substantive elements that are associated with the phrase in its public use. However, I think the phrase "Black Power" at least can be taken to represent appreciation of being a Black person in America and the demand by African Americans for the right of self-determination.

So understood I think that the Black Power movement can be said to be a morally healthy development. This does not mean that I think reconciliation among people is a bad thing. Nor do I mean to imply thereby that I am denying such values as equality and justice for the ordering of society. Rather it is to indicate the complexity of how such values are institutionalized and made efficacious in our society.

The Black Power movement has again taught us that unless we realistically and honestly examine our assumptions in the light of the concrete situation, our highest values may become but a way of blinding us to the injustice that we are helping to perpetuate. People of goodwill who call for reconciliation today between white and Black people in our society may be the Black person's worst enemy as the result of such moral idealism may well be to placate the African American demands at a level that will not radically change their disadvantaged position in our society. Moreover, the Black Power movement has also reminded the white liberal that good intentions are seldom adequate in the face of complex social wrongs. Phrases such as "all people are brothers" do little to affect actual life in the city ghetto.

In order that this positive evaluation of the Black Power movement might be more intelligible, it is necessary to make clearer some of my normative commitments. Presupposed in my judgment is the whole history of racism in this country that has resulted in the African American being systematically denied their right to full participation in this society in a way no other group has experienced. I therefore assume that the African American has a prima facie claim that the injustices of the past be rectified and their rights fully acknowledged.

Secondly, I am committed to the continued need to extend the participation of all people in a democratic society. All that is involved in the phrase "democratic society" cannot be analyzed here, but I understand it least of all to imply the procedure by which pluralism of group self-interests are tolerated to a high level in order to provide the conditions for greater equality and to seek through a balancing of these self-interests the greatest possible common good. Democracy is the attempt to provide an avenue of change by which these interests can find possibilities for greater justice without resorting to anarchy or excessive violence. (For a much more extensive and adequate analysis of Black Power from this perspective I highly recommend Joseph Hough's book *Black Power and White Protestants*.)

In this context I view the Black Power movement as a response by a minority to assure its participation in the society by organizing to protest its rights by power. It is a frank recognition that societies seldom respect the rights of the weak. Black Power, as I understand it, is thus not a phrase that is calculated primarily to scare white people, but rather a call from one African American to another that the goods of this society are theirs, not as they become what the white man wishes them to be but only as they become Black.

In this connection it is genuinely a mass movement, as it aims at equality for all African Americans—not just the talented few. As such it must be viewed as the real beginning of African American participation in our society. There is no doubt that this will cause extreme stresses in the established order of our society, but the development of justice seldom comes without tension. The moral substance of this development in this perspective in no way depends on the ethical goodness of the participants or their particular goals (just as the white participation does not), but rather should be regarded as an opportunity for the enrichment of our common social life.

Moreover, I think that the Black Power movement is morally sound as it perceives with greater clarity and honesty the role of power in group relations. No longer is the "goodwill" of white people depended on in their [African Americans'] calculations. Rather they have discovered that such "goodwill" can be relied on only to the point that it affects white self-interest. In response they have entered the arena of power by asserting their own voice(s) through candid and at times unrestrained speech. This seems to me to be a healthy reaction against some of the idealistic tone of the civil rights movement that was set by Martin Luther King.

The African American, in order to participate in our society and to assert their interests, is not required to have a higher moral excellence than the white American; nor is her mission the attempt to save the white from the prison of their prejudice. The African American can and should take part in our society in the pursuit of their own self-interests and goals by trying to ensure them through the same kind of power other groups in our society use.

Another aspect of the Black Power movement I find morally promising is the assertion of the right of participation in our society that envisages a way of life different from that of middle-class America. It is the claim that the African American has a special experience in America that they are intent on bringing into the future. This experience leaves them dissatisfied with the quality of life they see in wider society, and they are determined not to mimic it. I cannot help but think that the African American struggle to find a better way of life consistent with their experience will contribute immensely to the value of the American experience. It may even open for all of us further moral options that we had not before envisaged as possibilities for our lives.

Even though I have given a positive evaluation of the Black Power movement, there are some questions that I should like to raise concerning it in terms of its more specific manifestations and political strategies. Approval of the general thrust of the Black Power movement does not necessarily imply approval of all that is done in the name of Black Power.

The first question is whether it can accomplish politically what is required of it. It used to be a maxim among liberals that the action necessary to meet the needs of the African American and the poor could only be accomplished by a coalition of African Americans, poor white people, unions, and white liberals. The Black Power movement has decisively and perhaps rightly called that strategy into question.

It may be that the concentration of African Americans in American cities has provided the political opportunity for an African American declaration of independence. However, it is not clear to me whether Black Power alone is going to be able to provide the political leverage for the kind of help our cities currently need. Will it be necessary or possible for the African American to enter into coalitions with other groups in our society to work toward common political goals? Or will it be possible to determine "common political goals" from our mutual perspective?

This is not a question that is aimed at limiting the nature of the Black Power movement, but rather one that tries to ask, where do we go from here in order to meet our immediate needs? It may be that the best thing for the African American child in the ghetto is not integrated education, but that does not solve the problem of how that child can be provided with the kind of education they will need to compete in the modern world as an African American.

My second question has to do with a broader concern. "Black Power" is more than a political slogan. It is a phrase that denotes a search for identity with integrity on the part of the African American. This is an age in which all people are rather unsure as to who they are, and the African American search for identity is but a rather special case of this general problem. While I am in no way competent to judge how another can solve the question of their identity (if indeed such a problem can be said to have a solution), I am struck by a tendency that might prove dangerous in the long run for the Black Power movement; that is the assumption that to achieve political power can somehow satisfy the need for personal identity.

The political realm, while of utmost importance, has limits which make it a poor place to discover the ultimate significance of life. The achievements made in politics are put together by many compromises that simply cannot meet the criterion of ultimate legitimation and wholeness with which the question of personal identity seems to be so intimately connected. It may well be that as the Black Power movement develops it may find that its main contribution has been in the less sensational but perhaps more important areas of our lives together.

Where does this leave the white liberal? Does this mean that they simply become an anachronism in the light of these developments? While I think this need not necessarily be the case, I do think it means that white liberals must take this opportunity to seriously rethink their position. In a way, the white liberal is fortunate because the African American, by declaring independence, has created a new possibility of freedom for the white American.

White liberals have had an almost morbid fascination with their own guilt. They have cherished it as a way of assuring their moral identity in a world where moral problems are so complex; questions of responsibility and guilt are impossible to determine. It is tempting for the African American to use this guilt to underwrite getting "theirs" as though they are but another interest group, but they have now rejected this temptation to get on with the business of being African American. (They may have done this partly because they found how unreliable the guilty are as their guilt can turn all too quickly to arrogant self-righteousness.)

Just as the African American cares not whether the white person feels guilty or not, so the white American should quit worrying about the color of their skin. The African American has in fact said to white people, "Do not try to find out what it is to be a person by identifying with us for we will only be able to meet as people when you face honestly what being a person requires without me." As white people we should accept this challenge to turn to the moral possibilities of our future, which are far more interesting than the guilt of our past.

This new freedom, however, does increase the white person's responsibility. In a way, white people have been able, by their use of the "African American problem," to delay coming to grips with many of the hard moral questions facing them. Here they were able to find an issue in which the good and the bad seemed to be drawn with unmistakable clarity. By identifying completely with the cause of the African

American, the white Americans were able to provide themselves with a feeling of righteousness. They therefore did not feel compelled to raise morally significant questions about the quality of life they were building for themselves in general. As Christians we were able to assume that at least being Christian meant being "for" African Americans.

Now that the African American has refused to be the warrant for the white person's moral existence—now that they refuse to be our cause—we are forced to ask ourselves what kind of people we wish to be and in what kind of society do we wish to live. No longer can we assume that all that is morally significant in our life is how we feel about African Americans. If we seriously address ourselves to these questions of our future, we may find someday we are able to meet the African American as a brother or sister in a far more profound way than is now possible. For then we will have found that we must both meet as people that share the struggle of what it means to be human.

Thus I wrote in 1969.[5] As I confessed above, some of what I wrote fifty years ago is embarrassing. I wrote as a white person to white people, which, given that Augustana was primarily white, is understandable but still regrettable. There is, moreover, a presumptive air about the piece that is objectionable. An attitude of "I know better than you" pervades what I wrote. But write it I did, and I should have known better. There are no excuses.

Black Lives Matter

I think, however, that I got some things right in 1969 and even that some of the things I wrote remain relevant. The most important move I made, I believe, was the suggestion that African Americans have a story to tell that is particular to their lives and cannot be lost. One must be careful about how to say this, but the ambiguities surrounding "integration" come to a head when considering the importance of that particular story; that is, integration can threaten the story and memory of what it means to be part of a people who have suffered a terrible injustice, which means the reality of slavery cannot be lost. Yet African Americans have refused to let their extraordinary mistreatment drive them to nihilism. In fact, they have done the impossible, that is, in the face of white arrogance and power they have had children.

In an interesting way I think the call that "Black lives matter" draws on many of the same presumptions that gave birth to the "Black Power movement." The cry "Black lives matter" is meant to help African Americans recognize that they share a common story, that they need one another if they are going to survive, and they must always—with care—identify who their real enemy is. Of course that is not a new reality; it just happens to have become a dramatic reality captured by incidences that make visible the everyday brutality African Americans have to endure.

Just as it was true of the Black Power movement, some white people, including many who are very sympathetic with the cause of African Americans, find the mantra "Black lives matter" offensive. They call for the recognition that "all lives matter." That is, of course, true; all lives do matter. But to pose these statements as contrasting statements implies that white Americans feel threatened by the African American imperative to remember and tell their particular story.

"Black lives matter" is a cry that locates African American life in a history that is irreplaceable. By contrast, "all lives matter" fails to elicit the history that finds expression in the fear that fuels the white policeman's brutality toward African American males. At the heart of the problem of race in America, a problem I vaguely intimated in my essay on Black Power, is the inability of Americans to acknowledge that we are a slave nation. The Civil War, which is often appealed to as the price needed to be paid to end slavery, is not sufficient to make slavery "an unfortunate period in American history that we are now long past."

The American attempt to relegate slavery to "history" is a correlative of the moral inability to deal with slavery and subsequent racism. In this respect I think the civil rights campaign is now used by white people to justify our unwillingness to face morally what it means to be a slave nation. That failure results in what I call the failure of the success of the civil rights campaign. What could I possibly mean by that? I certainly do not mean that the gains made by Martin Luther King Jr. and those who followed him were not significant.[6] Without the civil rights struggle one cannot imagine that Obama could have been elected president of the United States. Yet I think I am right to suggest that the continuing inability of Americans to confront this nation's slave history, as well as the subsequent racism, is at least in some sense due to the successful failure of the movement for civil rights for African Americans.

By suggesting that the success of the civil rights movement has become a failure is my way of calling attention to the presumption by many white people in America that racism, or at least the effects of racism, has been overcome—if not eliminated—by the civil rights movement and subsequent legislation. Many assume that Martin Luther King won. He got the vote for African Americans, he is a national hero with a day set aside to celebrate his life, and African Americans now have the same opportunities to achieve a better life that white people have always had. Thus the assumption that African Americans can move to the suburbs, have nice homes with four bedrooms, three TVs, two cars, and worry about Jews moving in. Thus the presumption by white people in America that, given the success of the civil rights movement, what could be the problem with a little slavery/racism between friends?

To call attention to the "failure" of the civil rights struggle is my attempt to get at the mistaken presumption by many that the virulent racism in America is no longer a problem. The racism that dominates American life is all the more perverse because many now believe that America has come to terms with the reality that we are a slave nation. In short, the presumption that we have overcome slavery has now become part of the story of moral progress that shapes American self-understanding.

But slavery names a reality that is so wrong it feels as if there is nothing anyone can do to make it right. There is much to be said for reparations, but no compensation can compensate for the terror that was slavery.[7] I do not want to be misunderstood. I am not suggesting that racism is less a wrong than slavery. Racism can in fact be more insidiously destructive than slavery. I live in wonder that African Americans are not more filled with rage than they are for the everyday slights they receive for no other reason than the color of their skin. Knowing how to resist racism, moreover, must take more energy and skill than most of us can muster on a daily basis.

Yet I think it true that slavery, the presumption that another human being can be "owned" by another human being, was and is a monstrous practice. It is also wise to remember that slavery and racism each have economic outcomes. The economic character of racism is obviously different than slavery, but both entail forms of extraction of labor that result in keeping those who do the hard work poor. The economics of racism made racism a way of life that produced Jim Crow laws, justified white arrogance, and killed African Americans who were singled out for defying the system. It is probably true that racism is also an evil about which there is nothing that can be done to make it right.

There is a way to deal with a wrong that is so wrong there is nothing that can be done to make it right—it is called "forgetting." Perhaps the most effective form of forgetting is to regret that slavery ever existed but to celebrate that slavery was forever eliminated by the Civil War. Both the Civil War and the civil rights struggle are now seen as part of an ongoing story of progress that is thought to be the moral heart of America. I suspect there is no greater indication of the failed success of the civil rights struggle than how the results of the civil rights campaign are used as evidence against those who draw attention to the ongoing and pervasive racism that marks this country. The story of America's progress toward justice masks the reality that justice remains elusive for African Americans.

The crucial question, a question that I was close to asking in 1969, is, how do Americans come to terms with the reality that we were a slave nation without the telling of that story reproducing a progressive account of American history—that is, we once had slaves but we overcame that terrible institution? Joe Winters has recently written a book with the wonderful title *Hope Draped in Black: Race, Melancholy, and the Agony of Progress,* in which he argues that progress, even when used to galvanize struggles for a more just world, harbors a pernicious side by downplaying the tensions, conflicts, and contradictions in the effort to sustain hope for a better future. Progress turns out to be a form of forgetting just to the extent it relies "on the denial or easy resolution of painful tensions and contradictions in past and present, those facets of life that remind us that the status quo is harsh and cruel for many people under its sway."[8]

Winters argues that is why melancholy is a necessary trope for how the African American story is told. That story cannot be told truthfully without the inclusion of the "somber stories and songs" produced by slaves and which remain the heart of African American life. In particular Winters calls attention to W. E. B. Du Bois's use of the solemn songs in *The Souls of Black Folks* in an effort to resist having the striving of Black people absorbed into a progressive account of history.[9] The problem, from Winters's perspective, is that progress has become the condition of hope in America, which means there is no place for the melancholy that must suffuse the story of African American life if slavery is not to be forgotten.

Melancholy is the mood that names what it means to be unsettled and wounded by the unavoidable threats ever-present in human existence, that is, death, tragedy, and loss. Melancholy is a way of being in the world that does not attempt to wall the self from the everyday ways our life remains vulnerable and unsafe. Melancholy combines joy and sorrow, pleasure and pain, and in the process makes possible a hope that does not betray the reality that to be an African American means you inherit the sadness of a people who were enslaved.[10] Melancholy finds expression in the Psalms of lament.

Winters develops his argument by providing a painful account of President Obama's "A More Perfect Union" speech delivered in Philadelphia on March 18, 2008. Obama was responding to his former pastor, Jeremiah Wright, who had preached a sermon in which Wright called for God to damn America. Obama's speech, a remarkable speech in many ways, in a paradigmatic way is determined by the story of progress that Winters argues has become the basis for the hope for the end of racism in America. Thus Obama urges African Americans "to embrace the burdens of our past without becoming victims of our past." To avoid being victims Obama maintains that they "must always believe that they can write their own destiny."

According to Obama, Wright's mistake was to speak in a manner that assumes a static view of American society in which no progress has been made. But change has happened, Obama asserts, which indicates that the true genius of America is the audacity to hope for what can be and must be achieved. Winters acknowledges that Obama indicates that his political status and success do not signify that racism has come to an end, so there is a mournful and tragic sensibility that the speech exhibits. At the same time, however, Winters contends that Obama's "reflections tend to rely on a familiar logic of progress and a semantics of national exceptionalism that diminish attunement to race-inflicted loss, suffering, and struggle."[11]

Winters concludes his account of Obama's speech with the harsh but I think true judgment that Obama adopted the grammar of American exceptionalism, which has the effect of conflating hope and promise in a manner that assumes that the nation-state must be the agent of their realization. That mode of conflation, Winters argues, hides and minimizes the internal violence needed to secure the nation.[12] What is required according to Winters is a counternarrative that does not forget the solemn songs, the melancholic songs, that make possible the memory of slavery that renders the congratulatory progressive story of America problematic.

This account of the failure of the success of the civil rights movement may seem to continue the presumption that American politics will produce moderately progressive politicians who think it a "good thing" to find ways to continue to support the gains African Americans have made. But we know that assumption has now been decisively called into question by the election of Donald Trump to the presidency. Trump seems to have no understanding of what it means to be an African American in America. Nor does he seem to have any stake in the legal safeguards and social programs developed to help African Americans survive racism. Trump, moreover, has legitimated the return of a more overt racism that is as ugly as it is frightening. The gains made by the civil rights struggle cannot be lost.

Where Has This Gotten Us?

In his fine book *Bonhoeffer's Black Jesus: Harlem Renaissance Theology and an Ethic of Resistance,* Reggie Williams makes the judgment that Bonhoeffer "remains the only prominent white theologian of the twentieth century to speak of racism as a Christian problem."[13] The qualifier "prominent" makes his generalization true because Will Campbell, who spoke and wrote painful but true theological reflections on race, was not—nor did he wish to be—a prominent theologian.[14] But I believe it was from Campbell that I learned how to think about race theologically. For Campbell, racism is not just another sin; racism is a power that threatens our very existence as God's people.

The theology of my 1968 essay—to the extent it was theological—was basically that of Reinhold Niebuhr. I assumed some balance of power between groups was a given. But African Americans are not just another interest group. They are a people bound together by the story of their triumph over slavery and racism. That triumph I believe was made possible by the Christian faith African Americans received from slave owners, which made possible the miracle of lives that were not to be consumed by hate.

Theologically what is required is a determination by white people to remember the ugly history of slavery and racism. That is a story that can only be told as a confession of sin. But sin confessed makes possible a life no longer under the power of the dreadful need we have to justify the evil we do as good. Forms of penance offer ways that make kindness a possibility. For surely one of the most destructive aspects of slavery is how slavery made kindness an anomaly.

I think that Williams's charge that white theologians have failed "to speak of racism as a Christian problem" is not just a suggestion that theologians ought to be against slavery and racism. That is a far too easy stance. Given Williams's account of Bonhoeffer, moreover, neither is his call to think theologically about race satisfied by taking a liberationist perspective. Rather I take Williams to be suggesting that a theology which may in every way be orthodox will be less than it should be if it is done ignoring how it may be implicated in racist practices. Put concretely, the "very man" of the incarnational claim that Jesus was very God and very man threatens to become a very *white* man if salvation does not entail liberation from the prison of race.

I confess that I may be guilty of doing theology in a manner that fails to struggle against the inherent racism that can be present, present because absent, in what appears to be straightforward theological claims. The repair of Christian theology will not be accomplished by some of the familiar forms of identity politics because that kind of theology is the attempt to avoid what is most needed, that is, the truth. Rather we must begin by acknowledging that racism is an ecclesial sin that can only be dealt with by the gifts of the Spirit. If slavery is a wrong so wrong there is nothing you can do to make it right, the only alternative is to be drafted into a history of God's redemption that makes confession and forgiveness a reality. Only those who are willing to be forgiven can seek reconciliation with those they have harmed.

The church has been gifted by a story of a person whose death made possible the existence of a people that the world could not imagine. A church is made up of a people committed to sharing their stories, their lives, in the hope that through such sharing we might better understand who we are. To get our stories straight will require sharing our stories in a way that tests their truthfulness. For if I have any comment about the continuing alienation between white and Black people, it is that, finally, when all is said and done, the truth matters. That truth, a truth that is to be found hanging on a cross, makes hope possible even in the face of an ongoing injustice. Finally, the question must be, how are we to understand that in the years after the Civil War until our own day African Americans have most nearly been what we call "a Christian"?

10

To Be Befriended

A MEDITATION ON FRIENDSHIP AND THE DISABLED

In the communities of l'Arche we live and journey together, men
and women with disabilities and those who feel called to share
their lives with them. We are all learning the pain and joy of community life, where the weakest members open hearts to compas-
sion and lead us into a deeper union with Jesus. We are learning to
befriend them, and through and with them, to befriend Jesus.

—JEAN VANIER, *Befriending the Stranger*

On Changing the Subject

Jean Vanier begins his book *Befriending the Stranger* with these familiar reflections, at least familiar for anyone who has read Vanier. To
hear or read Vanier describe his friendships with core members of the
l'Arche communities is to be persuaded that he is describing authentic
friendships. But that he is so persuasive can make us miss the challenge
entailed in the attempt to describe what it means to be befriended by
people who are intellectually disabled. What follows is my attempt
to provide examples that describe what such friendships might look
like. In the process, what we mean by friendship may be transformed.

This is a tricky matter. To begin with examples might seem an attempt to avoid philosophical accounts of friendship that call into ques-

tion the possibility that the relation between the intellectually disabled and those who are not can be a genuine friendship. I am not avoiding argument; rather I am interested in allowing an account of friendship to emerge as an illustrative counterexample to such accounts.

The very descriptions we use to describe those who are intellectually disabled are part of the problem. As Brian Brock argues in his moving book *Wondrously Wounded: Theology, Disability, and the Body of Christ*, the description "disability" inevitably "smothers" the relationships that are essential for genuine human love and friendship.[1] Instead, Brock suggests we use the description "people who carry the label disabled" as an alternative to the unhappy description "the intellectually disabled." He does so because, as he points out, ironically the most severely intellectually disabled do not struggle with their disability because they "are wondrously free from pondering what others suppose them to lack."[2]

It is not clear whether or how those who carry the label "disabled" suffer or do not suffer from their disability. They suffer from the attitudes and behaviors of those of us who imagine how we would feel if we were them. In short, we project on to the disabled how we think we would regard our lives if we were disabled. We do so, however, as people who are not disabled. Thus the sentiment seldom said but often presupposed, "I would rather be dead than suffer from X or Y." But people who are mentally disabled are not people other than who they are and accordingly can and do enjoy who they are.[3]

Often present but unacknowledged is the role of fear in the relationship between persons with intellectual disability and those not so disabled. We are fragile creatures whose vulnerabilities produce fears that make our being befriended by the disabled frightening. Such fears remain in those who are befriended by the disabled. That is why, as I will suggest below, friendship must be communal because only a community that is made of those aware of their limits can create the peaceful space for all to flourish.[4]

Hans Reinders identifies another problem in his important book

Receiving the Gift of Friendship: Profound Disability, Theological Anthro-pology, and Ethics. We often assume the profoundly disabled will be cared for because by doing so those providing the care become better people. Reinders argues that such a justification is perverse because it is a denial that we—that is, each of us—receive our lives as gifts.[5] No human can merit a greater humanity for herself. And it is dangerous to suppose otherwise. We can become more human, but we cannot become better humans. The difference hangs on whether we receive our life as gift. Whether disabled or abled, we receive our humanity, and it is from this posture of reception that our shared human dignity springs.

Brock argues that his way of describing people who are intellectu-ally disabled is entailed by a theological perspective. He observes that Christian communities often offer rival understandings of the roles and gifts of those called to be the church. We should not be surprised, therefore, that the disabled have a role to play in God's story of his people. Brock's book is an extended exercise to perform that project by focusing on his Down syndrome/autistic sixteen-year-old son, Adam. Brock understands his task is to witness to Adam's witness by telling the stories of what it means for Adam to be "wondrously wounded."[6]

Brock is admirably clear that his argument is theological all the way down. Accordingly he understands the Christian gospel to offer a way of life that enables our ability to live as vulnerable beings who have made peace with our limits and are able to delight in the unexpected. Such a way of life can be joyous and free because we no longer seek to be gods but are content to be creatures whose flourishing does not mean that we will not suffer. As the stories of Scripture often make clear, it is through suffering that we discover our place in God's story.[7]

Brock's argument is quite clear: if we receive the friendship God offers us in the gift of people with intellectual disabilities, our under-standing of friendship will by necessity be enriched.[8] Also at stake is that what we mean when we say God may have to be rethought. Or perhaps better put, we may discover the radical implications of what we have been saying when we have been saying "God." It is not hard to sense that the work of Karl Barth has informed Brock's proposals.

What could I possibly mean by referencing Barth? Just this. That Barth's anthropology is Christological, which means to be human is determined first and foremost by the relationship that exists between God and each creature. A reminder that to be a human being is to be a creature. Joan O'Donovan rightly draws out the implication of Barth's position by observing that Barth was the champion of "those individual beings at the border of human life: the unborn child, the severely defective infant, the very old and senile, the comatose patient."[9]

Whatever one may think of Barth, it remains the case that most assume that friendship is not possible between people who are intellectually disabled and those who are not. It is hard to overcome the presumption that friendship in the most basic sense names a relation between people in which there is a reciprocal concern for the welfare of the other, and it is assumed that those who bear the label of being the mentally disabled lack the agency to be in such a relation.[10] This is compounded by the challenge of the unequal power relation between the mentally disabled and those who care for them. In his attempt to give an account of friendship that is lasting, Aristotle argues that a kind of equality constituted by virtue is required. That condition seems to make impossible friendship between people who are intellectually disabled and those who are not.

Vanier and l'Arche, as the passage with which I began intimates, challenge that judgment. Crucial for sustaining that challenge is that the assistants' task in l'Arche homes is to learn to be with rather than to do for those who are dependent on others. L'Arche is based on the presumption that the desires and wishes of core members have first priority, but it nonetheless remains unclear how such a transformation makes possible friendship between assistants and the core members.[11] Nonetheless, Vanier's friendships with the core members with whom he lives stand as a stark reminder that friendship between people who are intellectually disabled and those who are not is a reality. The question is how to describe and account for that reality. It is to that task I now turn.

Friendship: To Share a Common World

James McEvoy has provided an account of friendship that helps us see how friendship between people who are intellectually disabled and those who are not is possible. According to McEvoy, "dialogue is intrinsic to friendship because behind the dialogue of friends lies the natural aspiration to share the same world and to build upon it the same hopes."[12] The emphasis on communication may seem odd for an account of friendship with those who may be limited by their speech, but as I hope to show, the body can speak eloquently.[13]

We are, people who are intellectually disabled and those who are not, bodily beings who share a vulnerability that makes us storied creatures. Our bodies can be storied by friendships that are constitutive of the relationships that characterize the narratives that we call our lives. The telling of stories to one another turns out to be a crucial activity for making and sustaining friendship because it is through stories that we are able to recognize what it means to live in a common but complex world.

What this might mean has been displayed by Patrick McKearney. McKearney is an English anthropologist who lived for fifteen months in a l'Arche home in what he describes as a minor English city. McKearney begins his article, which is tellingly entitled "Receiving the Gift of Cognitive Disability: Recognizing Agency in the Limits of the Rational Subject," by calling attention to Peter Singer's argument that those who are mentally disabled lack the ability to be autonomous moral agents. Singer draws the conclusion that the intellectually disabled can or should only have limited moral worth to others.[14] McKearney notes that Eva Kittay has countered Singer's views by observing that people can learn to value others even if they are incapable of "giving back." Though McKearney thinks Kittay's response is strong, it does not sufficiently account for the agency the intellectually disabled in fact have.

McKearney argues against Singer, stating that while the core members may not be autonomous moral agents, they have an agency that is often not recognized because we fail to understand the different ways they inhabit the world. McKearney suggests that difference was recognized by Vanier, who began assuming his living with the intellectually disabled was a religious duty but discovered that he had become a friend with those with whom he lived (3). In short, Vanier had discovered they shared a common world.

McKearney observes that Vanier's assumptions about disability and vulnerability meant he could no longer see those with whom he lived as "problems." Neediness turns out to be a source of life-giving relationships. McKearney, who has a theological background, observes that once Vanier ceased being afraid of his vulnerabilities, he rightly began to understand that God comes to us not in our strengths but in our weaknesses and vulnerabilities.

McKearney confesses that he began his work in l'Arche with a presumption not unlike Vanier had at the beginning of his being with the men with whom he had been charged to live. That is, he assumed that the young women he encountered who were described as intellectually disabled were passive dependents without agency. Such presumptions were reinforced by his first encounters with the core members of the home in which McKearney was to live. There he encountered Rachel, who was making random hand gestures; Sarah rolling herself around and around in her wheelchair; and Martha, who spoke constantly but did not seem to make sense. McKearney assumed these women were incapable of active engagement with the world.

But McKearney came to see these young women in a very different light. He discovered they were exercising agency of a very different kind than that assumed by those of us who think we are in control of our lives.[15] To recognize the agency of core members requires training that comes from learning, as the core members must learn, that the essential dependent character of our lives does not mean we are without agency.

Such agency begins with the acknowledgment of our vulnerability. Such acknowledgment entails exercises such as asking the assistants to recognize their dependence on others. And that requires training if they are to discover the many ways they have relied on others to live out the gifts that have made their lives possible. These insights are tested by their being asked to reflect on the sheer difficulty of helping core members shower and dress in the morning. The difficulty of providing such "help" can serve to create in assistants the vulnerability that the core members already embody. McKearney quotes one of the experienced assistant's observation that "l'Arche was never about 'us' helping 'them' . . . There may be differences in our cognitive abilities, but no difference at all in our shared humanity" (6).

Stories about the relations between assistants and core members are crucial for the development of friendships. Meals often provide the context for the telling and retelling of stories about core members as well as stories told by core members. For example, Maria, a long-term assistant, tells the story of her early confrontation with Sarah, who could not verbally communicate. Maria was given the task of helping Sarah have a bath. This was no easy task. Maria confesses she did not know what she was doing, but she assumed that neither did Sarah know what was happening. Finally, after some time, Maria figured out what to do. She reports, addressing Sarah directly: "And you just sat there very patiently and quietly. When I finally worked out what the right thing to do was, you looked at me dead in the eye—and then you laughed at me" (7).

McKearney reports that such stories, which are often told many times, serve to challenge the preconceptions the assistants bring to their work. For the stories are often told by the core members in a manner that makes them active subjects "capable of authoring actions that affect others." Through these exchanges the core members' "gifts" of the heart are discovered. Among those gifts is their keen insight into those who care for them. Rayna, a very experienced assistant, told McKearney: "You can't hide your personality from people with learning disabilities. You have to open yourself. They find your weaknesses and strengths very quickly, and that confronts you with your own disabilities and inabilities" (9).

McKearney reports on the importance of the language of "gift" to describe core members. In particular, McKearney suggests that one of the aspects that "gift" names in the core members is a kind of unusual honesty. Hilary, one of the assistants, describes Sarah smiling and enjoying herself as she looks into a full-length mirror. She smiles because she thinks she looks amazing. Hilary reports she is far too self-conscious to smile at herself while looking in a mirror as Sarah does. She would be too afraid that others would find her behavior too self-involved. But Hilary says Sarah can enjoy looking at herself in the mirror because "she really loves herself, and she helps me to start loving myself" (10).

Sarah's gift of joy reflected by her image in the mirror is, according to McKearney, the source of a particular kind of agency that is easily overlooked. Sarah, and the other women in the l'Arche home, have the "gift of ignoring the judgments of others and loving themselves" (10). Because these core members are incapable of embodying some of the social and moral ideals that characterize the life of those of us who are cognitive abled, they can be particularly perceptive and honest. Sarah and her friends do not recognize that looking into a mirror and smiling at themselves might make them appear self-obsessed. Yet because they are not afraid of being so understood, they bring a spontaneity to their life that makes friendship possible.

McKearney observes that the descriptions of agency he has tried to provide reveal the paucity of our existing language for describing the possibility of forms of agency other than those forms assumed by people like Singer. McKearney, however, directs attention to Veena Das, an anthropologist of ethics who provides a different understanding of the self and ethics. Das argues that ethics is not so much about the technologies of self-making as it is "an attentiveness through which one ties one's own fate to that of the other." Ethics so understood means the moral life is not constituted by cognitive activity but rather is an "attitude to the soul" (a phrase Das attributes to Wittgenstein).

McKearney draws on Das's account to suggest that training in l'Arche teaches the assistants to see the intellectual disabilities of those with whom they live not as impediments for their acting morally but as enabling aspects of ethical interaction that is charismatic. Their lives have more in common with the unruly saints of the church than the rational moral agents of a Peter Singer. Those who have learned to be their friends value the way they transgress assumed norms of behavior and "express the value of a liminal community" (15).

Adam Brock's Witness

McKearney's stories are sufficient to sustain the point I am trying to make, but I cannot resist providing a brief account of Adam by his father. I cannot resist not only because Brock's account is theologically astute but also because I am Adam's godfather. I hope to say just enough to tempt you to read the book.

Brock wants us to see Adam as he has learned to see Adam. Such a seeing entails theological discipline in which we learn to use well the word "God." For, as Brock argues, God is not an idea or essence that can be extracted from events, but God is a name revealed in the drawing of a people into a congregation. The people of God have been called out of the world, which is organized by other names that refuse to acknowledge that human life is a gift from God. Adam is such a gift.[16]

Brock makes the striking observation that if the kingdom brought by Jesus is shalom, then Adam may be the healthiest person he knows. Adam is able to live without worry about the future. Secondly, there is no gap between what Adam says and what he does. He simply cannot lie even though he communicates through his body. When he puts his hand on a visitor's mouth, he is genuinely wishing them a good hello. He is, moreover, emotionally sensitive, often breaking into tears when his parents and brother and sister argue. He is, moreover, in constant enjoyment of other people.[17]

These are hard-won insights about Adam by his father. For Adam to survive has taken extraordinary sacrifices and tried the patience of his family. Yet Brock is surely right to suggest that when he is with

Adam, he cannot forget how different and beautiful the social order is to which Adam witnesses. Adam is content to be a creature who is able to inhabit a time and place that challenges the surrounding culture.[18] Surely one cannot help but desire to have such a friend.

Adam is a Christian. During worship he walks to the center of the church, the cathedral at Aberdeen, takes off his socks and shoes, sits rocking back and forth, swinging something repetitively in his hand and gutturally vocalizing, all the while sitting at the feet of the priest. His father observes that Adam ensures that St. Andrews is not a church for anyone who thinks that to worship God you must always be quiet.

Recently, on his fifteenth birthday, Adam was confirmed. Brock includes in his description of Adam's confirmation a letter I wrote in celebration of that event. I wrote:

> I only wish I could be there to witness your becoming a stalwart of the church. I put the matter that way because confirmation means the church will depend on you to be fully embodied in Christ. These matters are tricky because you have for some time represented Christ for the church through your dancing. Some may say that is a strange description of your presence in worship. You just cannot be still. But I have always thought when I have been with you in worship that you are dancing to the music God's angels make as they glorify God. My hunch is you were granted the grace to be closer to those wonderful creatures than those of us who are identified as normal and grown up. So on this wonderful day dance for the gathered body of believers because we all need the joy that animates your movements.[19]

Ending with Vanier

This brings me back to Vanier and the passage with which I began. One of the dangers Vanier's work represents is that Vanier's prose can invite the presumption that he is far too pious and idealistic. When Jean Vanier writes, "We all need to deepen our love for Jesus, hidden in those who are often unwanted," the temptation is to read such thoughts in a sentimental manner.[20] Yet as I suggested above, there is nothing sentimental about Vanier. The high humanism that shapes many views of the disabled is absent in Vanier because he does not engage in false stories about his friends. He knows his friends are sometimes difficult. Their demands will not allow sentimental claims about innocence.

In his book *Reconsidering Intellectual Disability: L'Arche, Medical Ethics, and Christian Friendship,* Jason Reimer Greig has developed the most complete account we have of Vanier's understanding of l'Arche as a school for friendship. Greig rightly argues that Christian friendship, and the description "Christian" he rightly assumes appropriate for Vanier's understanding of friendship, is not simply an interpersonal affair but is first and foremost a communal moral endeavor.[21] No rite embodies that communal aspect of friendship more fully, according to Greig, than foot washing. To have one's feet washed by a core member joins the bodily and social practices that make friendships in l'Arche between core members and assistants possible.[22]

The thick analysis Greig provides of friendship and in particular of the role of the body in l'Arche homes is confirmed by a story Vanier tells about a core member named Eric in his commentary on the gospel of John. Vanier had come to know Eric during a year when he was on sabbatical and living in the home for the profoundly disabled. So Eric and Vanier ending up in the same space. Eric had arrived at l'Arche when he was sixteen. The local hospital, a psychiatric hospital, would no longer care for him. He was blind, deaf, and he could not speak. He was not toilet trained. Vanier confesses he had never seen so much anguish in one person, particularly one so young.[23]

Reflecting on Eric, Vanier observes that many who come to l'Arche have "a broken self-image." In particular they sense they have been a disappointment for their parents whom they sense do not "want" them because of their disability. They cannot help but conclude they are without value, and, even more destructive, they draw the conclusion that they are not lovable. L'Arche is the way Vanier discovered that by welcoming the stranger as a potential friend, though they are in terrible pain, they discover they are able to bear the pain because they are valued and made beautiful by being cared for by friends.

Eric proved, however, to be a challenge. What it might mean for Eric to be loved simply did not seem to be possible. Vanier was not deterred. Though Eric could not see or hear, Vanier was sure he could be touched. That is what they did—day after day they held and washed his body with respect and love. Slowly but surely they were able to communicate with him and he communicated with them. He was able to befriend because he had been befriended.[24]

Vanier comments on this transition by suggesting that what Jesus commands us to do is be befriended by the weak, those in need, the lonely. For when the poor, the weak, and the lonely claim us as friends, they prevent us from falling into the trap of power—especially the power to do good. To be befriended by the poor and disabled saves us from the presumption we must save the savior and the church. To accept our own poverty, to become vulnerable by being befriended by those who are filled with need makes this prayer possible: "Dear God, I cannot do this on my own. I need your help."

I suspect some may find Vanier's relationship with Eric remarkable but believe there is no reason to describe their relation as a friendship. Yet given McEvoy's account of friendship as sharing a common world, I think it not unreasonable to accept Vanier's description of his relation with Eric as a friendship. Friendship comes in many different shapes and sizes. We inhabit many shared worlds. Moreover, it is surely the case that the relation of Eric and Vanier is not as strange as Thomas Aquinas's claim that God desires to befriend us.

According to Thomas, charity, God's unrelenting desire to love and be loved by us, makes possible "a certain friendship with him."[25] For God, like Sarah, McKearney observes, loves and is loved because God delights in the love that created us to be "us." Such love transforms what Thomas identifies as servile fear into filial fear that fears only losing our friendship with God—a fear that makes us no longer servants but friends with the One who alone is capable of transforming our vulnerabilities into love.

Friendship has always been a major theme in my work but has been more important in my life. So I need to close with these brief remarks. In 1970 I was hired to teach theological ethics at a school called Notre Dame. I had no idea what I was getting into, and I am sure I made many mistakes. But the people at Notre Dame befriended me, a loose-cannon Protestant, and in the process taught me how to be befriended. Which is but my way to say, "Thank you."

Advice to Christian Theologians

To be asked to advise anyone with the ambition of becoming a theologian in the Christian tradition is not a happy assignment. To be called to do theology is a happy calling, but given the current institutional realities, it is not going to be easy to do theology well. By "current institutional realities" I am thinking about the increasing loss of people identifying as Christians but also developments in universities that make theology an unlikely subject.

I am aware that what I have just written must seem a poor way to begin an essay designed to give advice to anyone who would desire to be a theologian. But I have to be honest about the challenges before those who want to be theologians. I suspect the character of theology, as well as the institutional place in which theology can be done, may well be quite different than it has been for the duration of my career.

I suspect I have been asked to provide advice because I seem to have done well enough. I am increasingly aware of how lucky I was to be a theologian both for the church and the university during the time I have worked. In an odd way, I was fortunate not to receive extended advice about how to be a theologian. And I was not smart enough to take advantage of any advice I was given. As a result, I took risks I did not know I was taking, and that proved to be a good thing.

For example, I was not told, as most young graduate students are now told, that I should only publish with a university press. My first book, *Vision and Virtue,* was published by Fides Press—a press that was not on anyone's radar as an important scholarly press. It was, moreover, a press connected with the Christian Family Movement, an organization begun by a wonderful CSC priest from Austria who had strong socialist inclinations. I did not know it at the time, but it was an honor to be published by such people.

I thought what was important was not who the publisher happened to be. What I cared about was sharing what I thought needed to be said. I probably had a higher opinion about what I had to say than was justified, but introducing Iris Murdoch to the theological world was not unimportant. I simply did not understand what might be called the politics of publishing, so I did not publish to get tenure. I wrote because I wanted to change the world. I am still trying.

Bill May, an eloquent theologian who taught at Indiana University and Southern Methodist University, in the process of giving advice to young academic theologians would distinguish between "writing in" and "writing out." He associated the former with discourse shaped by disciplinary habits that only insiders to the discipline could understand. As an alternative, he advocated the importance of learning how to "write out." By "writing out" he meant that we should be able to write in a manner that the nonacademic can understand. I have tried to follow his advice.

To write out means it is very important to have a reader in mind whom you want to engage. That may well mean that you will at times try to create a reader. That such work is necessary defies the often-made distinction between scholarly and popular theology. Any paragraph or book by Rowan Williams is sufficient to call into question that dubious distinction. Of course, that does not mean that a reader may not find difficulty with this paragraph, chapter, or book, but there must be writing sufficient to lead them on.

Please do not misunderstand. I am not suggesting that you do not try to have your book, which of course is your dissertation, published by a university press. Rather I am suggesting that it is a mistake to let the assumed scholarly standards defeat why you are called to be a theologian in the first place. I have directed a good number of dissertations. I have always given my students this advice—write about what you care about. Write about what fuels your passions. Without passion, theology can be a deadly discipline that kills the soul. Few sins are more deadly than making God boring.

I began this essay calling attention to the challenges facing anyone desiring to be a theologian in the world as we now find it. Yet I want to suggest that the challenges I named are also opportunities for the recovery of theology as a free discipline. The loss of the church's social and political status means theologians are free to think thoughts that were hard to think when Christianity was assumed to be the ethos necessary to sustain something called Western civilization. I am not suggesting that all that was done in that respect was without value, but I do think we live in a new day.

This leads me to give advice that may seem strange. I think it particularly important in our time for theologians to read in areas that are not explicitly theological. What I take to be odd about such advice is that given the challenges that make theology seem to be a problematic enterprise in the modern university, one would expect the emphasis should be on the intensification of theology as a self-justifying discipline. But when theology becomes a self-consuming artifact, it betrays its character as a discourse about all that is. If theology becomes just another course to provide information about an esoteric subject, then something has gone wrong.

I am asking for much by giving such advice. My advice is one way to encourage those beginning in theology to avoid what appears to be the "in" topic of the moment. That is a temptation hard to avoid, but there is a remedy for avoiding that pitfall—you will always need friends who will read what you write and then tell you the truth. Friends, moreover, may regard you quite critically, and you may return the favor, but then it is wise to remember that our enemy is more likely to tell us the truth than our friends.

Moreover, it is important to remember that many of your friends are dead, but they have left material that can help you avoid the parochialism of the present. No one can command knowledge of the whole Christian tradition, but to read the theology of the early church is a necessary exercise for the doing of theology. Their problems are not necessarily our problems, but that is why they are so important. They help us recover a theological imagination by forcing us to think differently.

I have recently been given the gift of quite literally being in conversation with friends. Brian Brock, who probably knows me better than I know myself, developed a series of questions about my work that have now been published under the title *Beginnings*. Sam Wells and I have been recorded in conversation about our work published in a book called just that, *Conversation*. I call attention to these books because I think they may provide an example of how theology might be done in the future. Moreover, both projects display how friendship is integral to the theological task.

Above I stressed the importance of theologians reading widely and for enjoyment. You never know what might stir your imagination. For example, one of the more popular essays I have written is on the novel *Watership Down*. If you can make theological hay off a book about rabbits, you have an indication that nothing is off-limits and anything is potentially of use. But it is important to note that I did not read the novel thinking it might be of use. It turned out to be a novel that exemplified the interrelation of political theory and the importance of narrative, which gave me the opportunity to say better what I had been trying to say. There is no better way to enrich theological imagination than to read Dante.

One outcome of the recommendation to read widely is its importance for your relation to other disciplines such as scripture and historical theology that are necessary if we are to do theology well. I think we are approaching a time when the current disciplinary divisions are beginning to break down. I take that to be a good thing, but it also means extra labor for the theologian. One of our weaknesses as modern theologians is our thin knowledge of Scripture. How to make Scripture integral to theological work as was done by the Church Fathers remains a challenge that will require imaginative responses in that we are not sure we know what such work will look like.

At the very least, in order to avoid letting the current disciplinary divisions determine how we should think, it is a good idea to read what your colleagues in the other fields read. This is not to manipulate your relationship with your colleagues. On the contrary, it is a condition necessary to sustain the kind of conversations that can produce thought.

Conversation with colleagues is very important, but I also urge you to think of your writing as an attempt to be in conversation with those you do not know. Over the years I discovered that by writing I found friends I did not know I had. By writing I was introduced to people who were thinking thoughts that were not unlike thoughts I was trying to develop. The result for me has been a continuing education that I believe has made me a better theologian. If I had to name one characteristic that has made what I have done possible, it is my assumption that there is something else I need to learn. I have never presumed my education is finished.

Which brings me back to the worries with which I began. Will there be a people left who care that the work of theology be continued? If such a people exist, will there exist institutional resources that make the work of theology possible? My answer to such questions is, I do not have the slightest idea how to answer either. But I suspect changes are coming that I cannot imagine. What I am sure about is that those who are called to the office of theology for the church will have to take the church seriously if the work of theology is possible.

It is no secret that when the university became the primary home of theology, theologians began writing for other theologians. I hope we might be in a time when theologians will find their primary home in the church. That does not mean that theology will need to be written in a popular style, although that is not always a bad idea. But it means that theology cannot be isolated from the practices that are constitutive of the Christian community. That will require those who would be theologians in the future to do their work as if their life depended on it. The latter is the most important advice I can give because it happens to be true, that is, our lives do depend on the subject that makes what we do as theologians so important and so hard.

On Writing Theology

I have often wondered what genres are best suited to the theological task in our day. The phrase "in our day" indicates that I do not think that there is one way to do theology that defies time and space. I take it to be a noncontroversial claim that theology has been done in many different genres, often depending on who can read and write. It is often forgotten that during most of Christian history most Christians could not read or write. Accordingly, theology was not written for anyone, but theology, which was often done in conflictual situations, might well be found expressed in the way a church is positioned. It is a theological statement that churches are positioned around an altar.

If there is a time and/or method that could claim to be *the* genre for theology throughout Christian history, the sermon seems the most likely form to claim that honor. That generalization needs to be qualified, however, for the simple reason that sermons come in many shapes and sizes. The rationalistic sermons of eighteenth-century England share little with most sermons characteristic of what passes for sermons in mainstream Protestantism in America today.

I have not only wondered and thought about which genres are

appropriate to theology; I have experimented by using different genres in what I have written. For example, I wrote a memoir, which is a genre that could only by the stretch of the imagination be thought to be a natural for theological reflection. Of course, whether a memoir can be theological will depend on how one understands what is meant by theology. The question of what constitutes theology is a subject for another day, but I do think the memoir is a tricky place to do theology.

My worry about the memoir as a genre for theological reflection is due in part to the unavoidable use of the first person singular in memoirs. When theologians give in to the temptation to use the genre of the memoir to do theology, they are often trying to explain what they take theology to be in self-referential terms. Thus the declaration by some theologians about what they are prepared or not prepared to believe. But if, as I believe, that theology is an office of the church, then a mistake has been made if the theologian thinks their subjectivity is all that interesting. But then there is that extraordinary book called *The Confessions* written by that person identified as Augustine, which surely qualifies what I just said. Yet it is not clear if Augustine's *Confessions* are a memoir. Moreover, it is the case that Augustine is Augustine and most of us are not.

Sermons, however, are another matter. I have delivered and subsequently published a fair number of sermons. But I suspect few would identify my sermons as the primary genre in which I have done theological work. I may, as I have often insisted, think some of my best theological work has been done in sermons, but I do not seem to have convinced many to think that is the case. But if one of the central tasks of theology is to comment on Scripture, the sermon is surely one of the genres necessary for that task.

There is, of course, also the commentary tradition, which is one of the primary genres for theology. It is the case when all is said and done that theology is exegesis of Scripture. It is a mistake, however, to maintain a hard distinction between sermons and commentaries given that the sermon, particularly before modernity, was assumed to be a commentary on Scripture in which theological work could be done. Of course, just as the sermon has taken on different forms throughout Christian history, so commentaries come in all shapes and sizes.

I have written a commentary on the gospel of Matthew. I confess I do not know how to characterize what I tried to do in that book, but I do know what I did was from the perspective of contemporary Old and New Testament critics more sermonic than scholarly. The critics are right to worry about my scholarly abilities because I certainly tried to write a commentary that called into question the presumption that to know what the text is saying the historical method must be used. Thus my refusal to use consciousness words that try to get you behind the text. For example, I avoided the grammar of claims such as "Matthew must have thought X or Y." Once you accept that convention of trying to get behind a text, you cannot help but give birth to misshapen questions about whether Jesus had a "Messianic Consciousness" and the equally misconceived "search for the historical Jesus."

The above remark about genres is simply my attempt to call attention to the diversity of forms that many of us have used to do theology. I am not sure, however, but I think what Brian has done in *Beginnings: Interrogating Hauerwas* may represent a genre of theological reflection that is a genuine alternative to our habits. I am not even sure I know how to describe the form that book took other than the description used in the title, that is, if it is anything, it is an interrogation. Interrogations are a relatively rare genre for theology, but I think it may increasingly become one of the standard forms theology takes.

I think it important to remember that genre issues have everything to do with the theologians' desire to be read. For some time, theologians have desired to be read primarily by other theologians, which has resulted in theology being weighted down with jargon. I take this to be an indication of what can be described as the academic captivity of the discipline of theology. I want to be clear that the scholarly character of theology done in an academic mode has been very important for helping us know how and even what we should think as Christians.

The genre for such theology is the monograph or the scholarly article. The articles are usually written by their authors to ensure that readers of the article will be people who write the way the author of the article writes. In other words, such articles are written to make Christians who are not academics know that they will never understand what Christianity is about.

The academic captivity of theology produces one of the most insidious dualisms that characterizes modern theology, that is, the distinction between theology that is popular and theology that is serious. The former is allegedly written for the laity, whereas the more serious theology is written perhaps for some clergy who still think they need to read theology but the implied reader is primarily other theologians. The deepest wound that results from the distinction between popular and scholarly theology is that the former often lacks substance.

Though I probably did not have a clear purpose in mind when I began to do theology, I did have the vague sense I wanted to defy the popular/scholarly alternative. Accordingly, I put in the same book a mixture of very different kinds of articles. Some of the chapters would only make sense if you knew something of the background issues that made the article read the way it must be read. Next to those chapters I would include an article on, for example, a book like *Watership Down*. It was my hope by doing so that some readers might see the connection between the more philosophical articles and those written for a wider readership.

At the center of my work has always been the role of language. My often-made formula—you can only act in the world you can see and you can only come to see by learning to say—I began to develop as early as *Vision and Virtue*. The formula is an extension of Ms. Murdoch's emphasis on description with an emphasis on the importance of language learned from Wittgenstein. But what I had learned from Wittgenstein also meant I had to avoid any attempt to write in a manner that "sums it all up." Therefore I sought to find a genre that is analogous to Wittgenstein's remarks. I have little stake in how you describe that genre, but I think calling what I have done "remarks" disguised as a book that is a "collection of essays" is probably as good a description that I can give.

I have not only used the article genre to subvert the popular/scholarly divide, but I have also written books not easily classified to undercut that alternative. These books are written to be read by interested laypeople. *Resident Aliens* is the best known, but to my great satisfaction I think some of the less-known works are perhaps more important. *Lord Teach Us* is a commentary on the Lord's Prayer, and *The Truth about God* is a set of reflections on the Ten Commandments. I mention these books because they are largely ignored by those in the more academic departments of religious studies and as well as seminaries, but I should like to think they have subsequent theological significance.

For example, in *The Truth about God* we argue that the interdependence of the commandments is a vital clue to help us understand why we need the concept "nature." For example, the command against stealing reflects the recognition that all that we have is a gift from God. Accordingly, nature is the term used to indicate that all that is that is not God is a reflection of the grace of God for that to exist that is not God. So Christian theology needs the concept of nature because nature names all that is by God's grace that is not God.

Above I called attention to the importance of sermons as a genre for theological reflection. I have published four collections of sermons. I regard them as some of my most basic and important work. Hopefully they manifest what I take to be the gospel. *Cross-Shattered Christ*, which is a book on the seven last words of Jesus, I believe to be some of the most haunting theological reflections I have tried to make articulate. It is my hope that these sermons as well as my commentary on the book of Matthew help my readers as well as this writer to live as people who believe that God is God and we are not.

In everything I do I try to make the familiar strange as well as help us awaken to the oddness of the everyday. Poetry no doubt is the genre that has at its heart that project. I do not pretend to have the talent of the poet, but I do try to make gestures that I should like to think have poetic effects. Those gestures are most determinatively found in prayer, which I take to be the genre that makes theology the praise of God. My little book *Prayers Plain Spoken* is my modest attempt to write in a genre that can be described as poetic. Some of the letters in *The Character of Virtue: Letters to a Godson* I hope have the humor that prayer makes possible.

Which finally brings me to try to say something about the imaginative alternative that *Beginnings: Interrogating Hauerwas* may be. The first thing that needs to be said, however, is that this is Brian Brock's book. He conceived it. He, along with Kevin Hargaden, did the hard work of organization. He did the even harder work of reading more of me than is probably good for anyone. He did so, moreover, without ever losing his own voice. That he always kept a distance gave the book a dramatic character because a reader hopefully cannot help but wonder where Brian is going to go next in his effort to force me to think thoughts I should or should not have thought given what I have thought in the past.

The genre of the book is unique because it is a conversation, but it is important that the unique character of that form not be overplayed if, I should like to think, everything I have said to this point suggests that theology is first and foremost a conversation. If you think that to be an exaggeration, think about prayer. *Beginnings*, therefore, simply makes explicit what I think should be the form theology should take when it is being done well. I am not sure I knew that before Brian suggested we do a book whose very form is a conversation.

My hunch is that one of the ways to make these observations about theology as conversations would be to attend to what Stanley Cavell calls "acknowledgment." As Toril Moi suggests in her recent book *Revolution of the Ordinary: Literary Studies after Wittgenstein, Austin, and Cavell*, by acknowledgment Cavell is not suggesting that acknowledgment is not a kind of knowledge but rather that it is the response required by knowledge. Acknowledgment is acting on knowledge. For example, I may know I am late for a meeting, but the knowledge that I am late does not entail my knowing I am late. Acknowledgment is the requirement that I reveal something about myself as a response to my being late. According to Moi, acknowledgment changes the dimension in which we assess our understanding of ourselves and others.

Just as I have deferred any attempt to define what theology is, so Moi resists any attempt to define "literature." Yet she suggests that Cavell's account of acknowledgment helps us understand why literary criticism is a conversation with the likes of a Goethe or Shakespeare. That is why it is impossible to write literary criticism without your own judgments being exposed. I take that also to be true for theology. That is why whatever genre theology may take, it cannot be anything other than a conversation initiated by God.

I need, moreover, to be perfectly candid. I had no idea what I was getting myself into when I responded positively to Brian's suggestion that we do a book in an explicit conversational mode. Kevin observes in his informative foreword to *Beginnings* the role of contingency in my work. If you ever want to know what contingency looks like, it was Brian getting me on board with this project. I had no idea that Brian Brock would seemingly from out of nowhere have the idea to produce a book like *Beginnings*. The only way I know how you might account for that is to tell a story about why he thought reading me with the care his questions exhibit is worthwhile. But surely that brings us back to the question of genre and in particular why Christian theology first and foremost takes the form of a narrative. So let me end with a grammatical remark that suggests why that is the case—"In the beginning, God."

NOTES

Introduction

1. Jennifer Herdt, *Forming Humanity: Redeeming the German Bildung Tradition* (Chicago: University of Chicago Press, 2019).
2. Herdt, *Forming Humanity*, 14.
3. Karl Barth, *The Humanity of God* (Louisville, KY: Westminster John Knox, 1960).
4. Karl Barth, *Against the Stream: Shorter Post-War Writings, 1946–1952* (New York: Philosophical Library, 1954).
5. Matt Jantzen, "Hermeneutics of Providence: Theology, Race, and Divine Action in History" (Th.D. diss., Duke Divinity School, 2017). Jantzen's work has been published under the title *God, Race, and History: Liberating Providence* (Lanham, MD: Lexington, 2021).
6. I am indebted to Darek Woodword-Lehman for his reading of Barth on practical reason. See his article "Reason after Revelation: Karl Barth on Divine Word and Human Words," *Modern Theology* 53, no. 1 (January 2015): 92–115.
7. The quote is from Andrew Errington's *Every Good Path: Wisdom and Practical Reason in Christian Ethics and the Book of Proverbs* (London: T and T Clark, 2020), 1.

1. The Christian Message in the World Today

1. Karl Barth, in the foreword to the Torchbook edition of *Dogmatics in Outline* (New York: Harper Torchbooks, 1959), 5, observes that the term "systematic

theology" is as paradoxical as a "wooden iron." I will comment further on this wonderful description in the next chapter.

2. Karl Barth, *Against the Stream: Shorter Post-War Writings, 1946–1952* (London: SCM, 1954); hereafter cited parenthetically in the chapter text.

3. Reinhold Niebuhr, *Essays in Applied Christianity*, ed. B. D. Robinson (New York: Living Age, 1959), 160. For a fuller account of the Niebuhr/Barth relation, see my "Karl Barth and Reinhold Niebuhr: Their Differences Matter," chapter 5 in this volume.

4. Niebuhr, *Essays in Applied Christianity*, 183–88.

5. Even as sympathetic an interpreter of Barth as Will Herberg thought Barth's silence on Russia, which in fact was not a silence, to be unjustified. Herberg observed that Barth's account of all-embracing grace led him to neglect difficult empirical analysis required for political judgments. As a result, Herberg argued, Barth's movement from theology to political decisions was beset with oversimplifications. See Will Herberg, "The Social Philosophy of Karl Barth," in *Community, State, and Church: Three Essays by Karl Barth* (New York: Anchor, 1960), 66. Herberg is quoting Charles West's account of Barth in West's great book *Communism and the Theologians*.

6. I am indebted to Mr. Matt Jantzen for directing my attention to the importance of *Against the Stream* in his dissertation, "Hermeneutics of Providence: Theology, Race, and Divine Action in History" (Th.D. diss., Duke Divinity School, Duke University, 2017). I have no idea how much of the following I learned from Jantzen, but I can only say he taught me much.

7. Jantzen, "Hermeneutics of Providence," 158.

8. Jantzen, "Hermeneutics of Providence," 168.

9. Justo Gonzalez, "The Reformation Isn't What It Used to Be," *Reflections* (Fall 2017): 24.

10. Jason Mahn, *Becoming a Christian in Christendom: Radical Discipleship and the Way of the Cross in America's "Christian" Culture* (Minneapolis: Fortress, 2016), 13.

11. Mahn, *Becoming a Christian in Christendom*, 18–20.

12. Karl Barth, *Barth in Conversation*, vol. 1, *1959–1962*, ed. Eberhard Busch (Louisville, KY: Westminster John Knox, 2017), 138–39.

2. The Christian Message, the Work of Theology, and the New Theology

1. Stanley Hauerwas, "Making Connections," in *The Difference Christ Makes*, ed. Charles Collier (Eugene, OR: Cascade, 2015), 77.

2. Bernard Lonergan, *Insight* (Toronto: Lonergan Research Institute, 2013), 3.

3. Karl Barth, *The Humanity of God* (Richmond: Westminster John Knox, 1963), 41.

4. For an account of the conference, see Eberhard Busch, *Karl Barth: His Life from Letters and Autobiographical Texts* (Philadelphia: Fortress, 1976), 366–67.

5. Karl Barth, *Against the Stream: Shorter Post-War Writings, 1946–1952* (London: SCM, 1954), 183; hereafter cited parenthetically in the chapter text.

6. Barth, *The Humanity of God*, 39.

7. Stanley Hauerwas, *With the Grain of the Universe: The Church's Witness and Natural Theology* (Grand Rapids, MI: Brazos, 2001), 173.

8. Toril Moi, *Revolution of the Ordinary: Literary Studies after Wittgenstein, Austin, and Cavell* (Chicago: University of Chicago Press, 2017); hereafter cited parenthetically in the chapter text.

9. For an excellent account of Wittgenstein's use of Augustine, see David Stern, *Wittgenstein's Philosophical Investigations: An Introduction* (Cambridge: Cambridge University Press, 2004), 72–87.

10. Ludwig Wittgenstein, *Philosophical Investigations*, trans. Elizabeth Anscombe (Oxford: Blackwell, 2001), 43.

11. Stanley Cavell, *The Claim of Reason: Wittgenstein, Skepticism, Morality, and Tragedy* (Oxford: Oxford University Press, 1979), 172.

12. Karl Barth, *Church Dogmatics*, 4/3 (Edinburgh: T and T Clark, 1961), 113.

13. Jonathan Tran, "Linguistic Theology: Completing Post-liberalism's Linguistic Task," *Modern Theology* 33, no. 1 (2017): 4.

14. Karl Barth, *Dogmatics in Outline* (New York: Harper, 1959), 5.

15. Barth, *Dogmatics in Outline*, 30–31.

16. Barth, *Dogmatics in Outline*, 22.

17. Barth, *Dogmatics in Outline*, 36–37.

18. Barth, *Dogmatics in Outline*, 31.

3. The Church and Civil Society

1. I use the phrase "the realist expression of the social gospel" to suggest that Reinhold Niebuhr, in spite of his fierce criticism of the social gospel, stands in that tradition. For the development of that argument, see my *A Better Hope: Resources for a Church Confronting Capitalism, Democracy, and Postmodernity* (Grand Rapids, MI: Brazos, 2000), 55–108.

2. Karl Barth, *Against the Stream: Shorter Post-War Writings, 1946–52*, ed. Ronald Gregor Smith (London: SCM, 1954), 13–50; hereafter cited parenthetically in the chapter text.

3. Karl Barth, *Community, State, and Church*, introd. Will Herberg (Garden City, NY: Anchor, 1960). The other essays that made up this book were "Gospel and Law" and "Church and State." I will reference these essays from time to time.

4. George Hunsinger, conclusion to *Karl Barth and Radical Politics* (Philadelphia: Westminster, 1976), 181.

5. Quoted in Hunsinger, *Karl Barth and Radical Politics*, 181.

6. See, for example, Timothy Gorringe's fine book *Karl Barth: Against Hegemony* (Oxford: Oxford University Press, 1999) for a detailed account of Barth's political activity.

7. As I suggested in an earlier lecture, I am concentrating on the occasional essays in *Against the Stream* because I am convinced that Matt Jantzen is right that Barth intentionally minimized explicit discussions of contemporary events in the *Church Dogmatics,* preferring to address concrete political matters in sermons, lectures, and letters. See Jantzen, "Hermeneutics of Providence: Theology, Race, and Divine Action" (Th.D. diss., Duke Divinity School, 2017), 134.

8. Bonhoeffer, from the beginning to the end of his life, was about the recovery of the church's visibility. I try to make that argument in *Performing the Faith: Bonhoeffer and the Practice of Nonviolence* (Grand Rapids, MI: Eerdmans, 2004).

9. Barth, *Community, State, and Church,* 120.

10. Barth, *Community, State, and Church,* 131.

11. Barth, *Community, State, and Church,* 132.

12. Barth develops these analogies in *Against the Stream,* 33–44.

13. Todd Cioffi, "Stanley Hauerwas and Karl Barth: Matters of Christology, Church, and State," in *Karl Barth and American Evangelicals,* ed. Bruce McCormack and Clifford Anderson (Grand Rapids, MI: Eerdmans, 2011), 363.

14. Robert Dean, *For the Life of the World: Jesus Christ and the Church in the Theologies of Dietrich Bonhoeffer and Stanley Hauerwas* (Eugene, OR: Pickwick, 2016), 12.

4. Reinhold Niebuhr

1. Stanley Hauerwas, *With the Grain of the Universe: The Church's Witness and Natural Theology* (Grand Rapids, MI: Brazos, 2001), 128.

2. Hauerwas, *With the Grain of the Universe,* 131.

3. Raymond Geuss, *A World without Why* (Princeton, NJ: Princeton University Press, 2014).

4. For my discussion of this claim, see *With the Grain of the Universe,* 55–58.

5. Langdon Gilkey, *On Niebuhr: A Theological Study* (Chicago: University of Chicago Press, 2001), xi.

6. Gilkey, *On Niebuhr,* 5–7.

7. Gilkey, *On Niebuhr,* 8–9.

8. Gilkey, *On Niebuhr,* 10–11.

9. Gilkey, *On Niebuhr,* 11.

10. Reinhold Niebuhr, *Beyond Tragedy: Essays on the Christian Interpretation of History* (New York: Scribner's Sons, 1937), ix.

11. Niebuhr, *Beyond Tragedy,* 205.

12. Niebuhr, *Beyond Tragedy,* 212.

13. Bernard Longergan, *Insight* (Toronto: Lonergan Research Institute, 1992), 3.

14. Abraham Heschel, *The Prophets: An Introduction* (New York: Harper and Row, 1955), xii.

15. Reinhold Niebuhr, *The Nature and Destiny of Man* (New York: Scribner's, 1949), 234.

16. Niebuhr, *The Nature and Destiny of Man*, 239.

17. Hauerwas, *With the Grain of the Universe*, 120.

18. Reinhold Niebuhr, *The Children of Light and the Children of Darkness* (New York: Scribner's, 1944), xi.

5. Karl Barth and Reinhold Niebuhr

1. Reinhold Niebuhr, *Essays in Applied Christianity,* ed. D. B. Robinson (New York: Meridian, 1959), 144.

2. Eberhard Busch, *Karl Barth: His Life from Letters and Autobiographical Texts,* trans. John Bowden (Philadelphia: Fortress, 1975), 342.

3. Niebuhr, *Essays in Applied Christianity*, 144.

4. Niebuhr, *Essays in Applied Christianity*, 144.

5. Niebuhr, *Essays in Applied Christianity*, 147.

6. Niebuhr, *Essays in Applied Christianity*, 148.

7. Reinhold Niebuhr, *Radical Religion* (1938); pagination is not available.

8. Niebuhr, *Essays in Applied Christianity*, 166–67.

9. Arthur C. Cochrane, *The Church's Confession under Hitler* (Philadelphia: Fortress, 1962), 240.

10. Karl Barth, "No Christian Marshall Plan," *Christian Century* (1948): 1333.

11. Barth, "No Christian Marshall Plan," 1330–31.

12. Barth, "No Christian Marshall Plan," 1332.

13. Gary Dorrien, *The Barthian Revolt in Modern Theology* (Louisville, KY: Westminster John Knox, 2000), 135.

14. Niebuhr, *Essays in Applied Christianity*, 172.

15. Niebuhr, *Essays in Applied Christianity*, 171.

16. Niebuhr, *Essays in Applied Christianity*, 174–75.

17. Karl Barth, "Continental vs. Anglo-Saxon Theology," *Christian Century*, February 16, 1949, 201–4.

18. Barth, "Continental vs. Anglo-Saxon Theology," 203.

19. Karl Barth, *Community, State, and Church*, introd. Will Herberg, (New York: Doubleday, 1960), 118.

20. Barth, *Community, State, and Church*, 149–89.

21. George Hunsinger, *How to Read Karl Barth: The Shape of His Theology* (New York: Oxford, 1991), 38.

22. Hunsinger, *How to Read Karl Barth*, 39.

23. Niebuhr, *Essays in Applied Christianity*, 182.

24. Niebuhr, *Essays in Applied Christianity*, 169.

25. Charles Brown, *Niebuhr and His Age* (Philadelphia: Trinity, 1992), 145.

26. Karl Barth, *Against the Stream: Shorter Post-War Writings, 1946–52* (London: SCM, 1954), 106–13.

27. Barth, *Against the Stream*, 113–18.

28. Niebuhr, *Essays in Applied Christianity*, 183–90.

29. Barth, *Against the Stream,* 185–86.
30. Brandon Morgan, "The Lordship of Christ and the Gathering of the Church: Hauerwas's Debts to the 1948 Barth-Niebuhr Exchange," *Conrad Gebel Review* 33, no. 1 (Winter 2015): 1–15.

6. God and Alasdair MacIntyre

1. Alasdair MacIntyre, *Whose Justice? Which Rationality?* (Notre Dame, IN: University of Notre Dame Press, 1988), 10.
2. Nussbaum wrote a stinging critique of *Whose Justice? Which Rationality?* in the *New York Review of Books* (December 7, 1989) in which she argued that she could not see how MacIntyre could sustain his call for a return to the locality as a Catholic Christian. She observes that no moral system has exterminated local traditions more relentlessly than Christianity, particularly in its Roman Catholic version. I take that to be an empirical claim that can invite an interesting exchange. She also challenged MacIntyre's use of the Christian understanding of original sin because "sin" is not a philosophical concept. I find that point quite interesting given MacIntyre's use of Augustine on original sin in *Whose Justice? Which Rationality?*
3. Alasdair MacIntyre, "Catholic Universities: Dangers, Hopes, and Fears," in *Higher Learning and Catholic Tradition,* ed. Robert Sullivan (Notre Dame: University of Notre Dame Press, 2001), 5.
4. Alasdair MacIntyre, prologue to *After Virtue: A Study in Moral Theory* (Notre Dame: University of Notre Dame Press, 2007), x–xi.
5. I once asked Alasdair what he makes of Aquinas on the "infused moral virtues." He said he tries not to think about them.
6. Alasdair MacIntyre, "What Has Christianity to Say to the Moral Philosopher?," John Coffin Memorial Lecture in Christian Ethics, University of London, May 21, 1998, 19. As far as I know this lecture has not been published.
7. Alasdair MacIntyre, "An Interview with Giovanna Borradori," in *The MacIntyre Reader,* ed. Kelvin Knight (Notre Dame, IN: University of Notre Dame Press, 1998), 265.
8. MacIntyre, "An Interview with Giovannaa Borradori," 266.
9. Alasdair MacIntyre, *God, Philosophy, Universities: A Selective History of the Catholic Philosophical Tradition* (New York: Sheed and Ward, 2009), 25.
10. MacIntyre contends rightly that every theology presupposes a set of philosophical positions, which means every theologian and priest must be philosophically educated. In the process, theologians need to be knowledgeable of the concepts through which the faith is articulated (*God, Philosophy, Universities,* 168).
11. MacIntyre, *God, Philosophy, Universities,* 166.
12. In the article "Truth as a Good: A Reflection on *Fides et Ratio,*" MacIntyre comments that it is not that the encyclical both presents certain philosophical positions with regard to truth and maintains the autonomy of philosophy, but rather

it is because the encyclical takes the view of truth it does, as well as sustaining the view that human beings are truth seekers, that the encyclical is committed to the autonomy of philosophy (Alasdair MacIntyre, *The Tasks of Philosophy: Selected Essays*, vol. 1 [Cambridge: University of Cambridge Press, 2006], 213).

13. Alasdair MacIntyre, *Three Rival Versions of Moral Enquiry: Encyclopedia, Genealogy, and Tradition* (Notre Dame, IN: University of Notre Dame Press, 1990).

14. Alasdair MacIntyre, "Preface to the1970 Edition," *Metaphysical Beliefs* (New York: Schocken, 1970), x.

15. MacIntyre, "Preface to the 1970 Edition," x–xi.

16. Alasdair MacIntyre, "Is Understanding Religion Compatible with Believing?" in *Faith and the Philosophers,* ed. John Hick (London: Macmillan, 1964), 132.

17. In a 1961 article entitled "Marxists and Christians," MacIntyre observed that what Marxists have to face about Christianity is the politically ambiguous character of Christianity. At the same time, some Christians could liken the sufferings of King Charles I to the sufferings of Christ the King while some Christians called Levellers were preparing to institute Christ's kingdom. The challenge before Christians from a Marxist point of view, therefore, is that Christians inherit from their past a radical stance that cannot be realized in the structures of capitalism. This article can now be found in *Alasdair MacIntyre's Engagement with Marxism,* ed. Paul Blackledge and Neil Davidson (Chicago: Haymarket, 2005), 179–86.

18. Alasdair MacIntyre, *Secularization and Moral Change* (Oxford: Oxford University Press, 1967), 32.

19. Alasdair MacIntyre, *A Short History of Ethics* (New York: Collier, 1966), 115.

20. MacIntyre, introduction to *Marxism and Christianity* (London: Duckworth, 1995), xx.

21. MacIntyre, "An Interview with Giovanna Borradori," 257.

22. MacIntyre, introduction to *Marxism and Christianity,* xx.

23. MacIntye, *Marxism and Christianity,* 112–13.

24. Alasdair MacIntyre, *Secularization and Moral Change* (Oxford: Oxford University Press, 1967), 67–68.

25. MacIntyre, *Secularization and Moral Change,* 68–69.

26. Alasdair MacIntyre, *The Religious Significance of Atheism* (New York: Columbia University Press, 1969), 24.

27. MacIntyre, *The Religious Significance of Atheism,* 25–26.

28. MacIntyre, *The Religious Significance of Atheism,* 28–29. MacIntyre has a very interesting manuscript from 1998 entitled "Three Kinds of Atheism" in which he argues that Nietzsche represents the most important atheist's challenge. As far as I know the paper has never been published.

29. MacIntyre, *The Religious Significance of Atheism,* 69–70.

30. MacIntyre, *God, Philosophy, Universities,* 5.

31. MacIntyre, *God, Philosophy, Universities,* 7.

32. MacIntyre, *God, Philosophy, Universities,* 8.

33. Alasdair MacIntyre, "Three Kinds of Atheism," manuscript, 1998, 21.

34. MacIntyre, *God, Philosophy, Universities*, 38.

35. MacIntyre, *God, Philosophy, Universities*, 41.

36. Alasdair MacIntyre, *Ethics in the Conflicts of Modernity: An Essay on Desire, Practical Reasoning, and Narrative* (Cambridge: Cambridge University Press, 2016), 315.

37. MacIntyre, *God, Philosophy, Universities*, 141–42.

38. Karl Barth, *Anselm: Fides Quaerens Intellectum* (New York: Living Age, 1962), 99. I am indebted to Steve Long for reminding me of this statement by Barth.

39. Alasdair MacIntyre, "On Being a Theistic Philosopher in a Secularized Culture," *Proceedings of the ACPA* 84 (2011): 23.

40. MacIntyre, "On Being a Theistic Philosopher," 25.

41. MacIntyre, "On Being a Theistic Philosopher," 25.

42. MacIntyre, "On Being a Theistic Philosopher," 25.

43. MacIntyre, "On Being a Theistic Philosopher," 29–30.

44. Alasdair MacIntyre, "Intractable Moral Disagreements," in *Intractable Disputes about the Natural Law: Alasdair MacIntyre and Critics*, ed. Lawrence Cunningham (Notre Dame, IN: University of Notre Dame Press, 2009), 26.

45. Alasdair MacIntyre, "From Answers to Questions," in *Intractable Disputes about the Natural Law: Alasdair MacIntyre and Critics*, ed. Lawrence Cunningham (Notre Dame, IN: University of Notre Dame Press, 2009), 315.

46. In an article on the work of Rabbi Jonathan Sacks, MacIntyre explicitly invokes the work of David Novak to underwrite the place of the Noahide laws, which Maimonides defended as based on reason and not on God's commands. MacIntyre observes that Novak distinguishes reasons based on reason from reasons based on a specific history. MacIntyre argues, however, that the universality of the prohibitions in the Noahide code are learned not by being universal but by being particular. MacIntyre quotes Sacks's claim that "we learn to love humanity by loving specific human beings," but he argues that we dare not forget that those human beings who come often do so as strangers who are subject to the Noahide law. MacIntyre's essay is in *Radical Responsibility: Celebrating the Thought of Chief Rabbi Lord Jonathan Sacks*, ed. Michael Harris, Daniel Rynhold, and Tamra Wright (London: Maggid, 2013), 3–16.

47. Alasdair MacIntyre, "Natural Law as Subversive: The Case of Aquinas," in *Ethics and Politics: Selected Essays* (Cambridge: Cambridge University Press, 2006), 62–63.

48. Alasdair MacIntyre, "Address Delivered at the Inauguration of Paul Joseph Philibert," (1987), 15–16. As far as I know, this lecture has not been published. I think MacIntyre's emphasis on the contingent beginning of every tradition has not been appropriately appreciated for how he understands the importance of change for individuals and communities. See *Whose Justice? Which Rationality?* (Notre Dame, IN: University of Notre Dame, 1988), 354–57. MacIntyre's relation to the work of Herbert McCabe and Fergus Kerr would make a fascinating study in this respect. In particular, how Wittgenstein has shaped their understanding of a tradition-determined rationality would be extremely informative.

49. MacIntyre, "Address Delivered," 17. Just on the off chance some might miss my stake in this reading of MacIntyre, I should like to think this way of construing MacIntyre's position is not dissimilar to the argument I tried to make in *With the Grain of the Universe: The Church's Witness and Natural Theology* (Grand Rapids, MI: Brazos, 2001).

7. Wounded

1. The meeting was the idea of Bishop George Sumner of the Diocese of Dallas. Speakers were to explore the challenges before those in the priesthood. It was hoped by doing so some would be attracted to the priesthood. The meeting was at the Church of the Incarnation in Dallas in 2018.
2. Stanley Hauerwas, "Making Connections," in *The Difference Christ Makes*, ed. Charlie Collier (Eugene, OR: Cascade, 2015), 77.
3. Samuel Wells, *Incarnational Ministry: Being with the Church* (Grand Rapids, MI: Eerdmans, 2017), 168–84.
4. Christopher Beeley, *Leading God's People: Wisdom from the Early Church for Today* (Grand Rapids, MI: Eerdmans, 2012), 108. Will Willimon rightly maintains in his *Pastor: The Theology and Practice of Ordained Ministry* (Nashville: Abingdon, 2002) that the great challenge is to care for the wounded in the manner of Christ. Accordingly, he has some quite critical things to say about CPE (171–98).
5. For a fuller working out of this contention, see Stanley Hauerwas, *Christian Existence Today: Essays on Church, World, and Living in Between* (1988; Grand Rapids, MI: Brazos, 2001), 149–70.
6. Sarah Coakley, "Can Systematic Theology Become 'Pastoral' Again, and Pastoral Theology 'Theological'?," Australian Broadcasting Company "Religion and Ethics," July 24, 2017, www.abc.net.au/religion/can-systematic-theology-become -pastoral-again-and-pastoral-theol/10095582.
7. William Clebsch and Charles Jackle, *Pastoral Care in Historical Perspective* (New York: Jason Aronson, 1983); G. R. Evans, ed., *A History of Pastoral Care* (London: Cassell, 2000).
8. Clebsch and Jackle, *Pastoral Care in Historical Perspective*, 13.
9. Clebsch and Jackle, *Pastoral Care in Historical Perspective*, 8–10.
10. Clebsch and Jackle, *Pastoral Care in Historical Perspective*, viii.
11. H. Richard Niebuhr, *The Purpose of the Church and Its Ministry* (New York: Harper and Row, 1956), 76.
12. Alasdair MacIntyre, *After Virtue*, 3rd ed. (Notre Dame, IN: University of Notre Dame Press, 2007), 30.
13. Alasdair MacIntyre, *Ethics in the Conflicts of Modernity: An Essay on Desire, Practical Reasoning, and Narrative* (Cambridge: Cambridge University Press, 2016), 123.
14. Adrian Pabst, "'Ware of Position': Liberal Interregnum and the Emergent Ideologies," *Telos* 183 (Summer 2018): 192.

15. For a critique of Tillich's understanding of pastoral theology, see Deborah Hunsinger, *Theology and Pastoral Counseling: A New Interdisciplinary Approach* (Grand Rapids, MI: Eerdmans, 1995), 88–95.

16. Stephen Pattison, *A Critique of Pastoral Care* (London: SCM, 1988), 40–41.

17. Pattison, *A Critique of Pastoral Care*, 38.

18. Joseph Fletcher, *Situation Ethics: The New Morality* (Philadelphia: Westminster, 1966), 164–65.

19. Pattison, *A Critique of Pastoral Care*, 30–31.

20. Hunsinger, *Theology and Pastoral Counseling* vii; hereafter cited parenthetically in the chapter text.

21. Karl Barth, *Final Testimonies* (Eugene, OR: Wipf and Stock, 2003), 23.

22. Barth, *Final Testimonies*, 24.

23. Karl Barth, *God in Action* (Eugene, OR: Wipf and Stock, 2005), 12.

24. Barth, *God in Action*, 15.

25. Barth, *God in Action*, 19.

26. Barth, *God in Action*, 23.

27. Barth, *God in Action*, 27.

28. Barth, *God in Action*, 28.

8. The Church in Asia

1. I wrote this lecture for a meeting sponsored by Duke Divinity School and the Mennonite Central Committee to explore challenges facing the Christian movement in Asia. The meeting took place in Japan in 2017.

2. For example, I was recently made aware of the controversies surrounding my work by Wenjuan Zhao, whose graduate work centered on my work. She also directed my attention to the essays by Lap Yan Kung and Sam Tsang in the book *Asian Christianity in the Diaspora* (New York: Palgrave, 2016), in which my work was discussed.

3. For a keen assessment of the current status of Christendom, see Jason A. Mahn, *Becoming a Christian in Christendom: Radical Discipleship and the Way of the Cross in America's "Christian" Culture* (Minneapolis: Fortress, 2016).

4. Bruce Kaye, *The Rise and Fall of English Christendom: Theocracy, Christology, Order and Power* (London: Routledge, 2018), vii.

5. Kaye, *The Rise and Fall of English Christendom*, 31.

6. It is often forgotten that before the description "globalization" became the key word, we had another way to speak of a more interdependent world—we called it Catholic.

7. Kaye, *The Rise and Fall of English Christendom*, 27.

8. Kaye, *The Rise and Fall of English Christendom*, 28.

9. Dana Robert, *Christian Mission: How Christianity Became a World Religion* (Oxford: Wiley-Blackwell, 2009), 49.

10. Robert, *Christian Mission*, 69.

11. Robert, *Christian Mission*, 93.

12. Peter Leithart, *The End of Protestantism: Pursuing Unity in a Fragmented Church* (Grand Rapids, MI: Brazos, 2016), 86.

13. Leithart, *The End of Protestantism*, 84.

14. Leithart, *The End of Protestantism*, 144.

15. Leithart, *The End of Protestantism*, 180–81.

16. Chloe Starr, *Chinese Theology: Text and Context* (New Haven, CT: Yale University Press, 2016), 185–212.

17. I worry that this focus on developments in China may give the impression that Christianity in China, given the numbers, is more important than developments elsewhere in Asia. I certainly do not think that to be the case. I am also aware that the house church/Three-Self Movement divide does not do justice to the complexity of Chinese Christianity. As Nanlai Cao argues, the dichotomous view of state domination and church resistance certainly does not do justice to the "Boss Christianity" of Wenzhou. See her *Constructing China's Jerusalem: Christians, Power, and Place in Contemporary Wenzhou* (Stanford, CA: Stanford University Press, 2011), 163.

18. Starr, *Chinese Theology*, 185.

19. The Three-Self Movement was the Chinese government's sponsored form of Christianity in which the churches were to claim their independence from the "imperialism" of missionary agencies. The Three-Self churches were to be self-supporting, self-governing, and self-propagating.

20. For a good study of Wang Mingdao, see Thomas Alan Harvey, *Acquainted with Grief: Wang Mingdao's Stand for the Persecuted Church in China* (Grand Rapids, MI: Brazos, 2002). I was Dr. Harvey's dissertation director, which means he gave me a wonderful education about the church struggle in China.

21. Starr, *Chinese Theologians*, 185.

22. Starr, *Chinese Theologians*, 188.

23. Kaye, *The Rise and Fall of English Christendom*, 31.

24. Starr, *Chinese Theologians*, 194.

25. Starr, *Chinese Theology*, 207–8.

26. Karl Barth, *Against the Stream: Shorter Post-war Writings, 1946–52* (London: SCM, 1954), 81.

27. Barth, *Against the Stream*, 34.

28. Kaye, *The Rise and Fall of English Christendom*, 294.

29. Kaye, *The Rise and Fall of English Christendom*, 283.

30. Kaye, *The Rise and Fall of English Christendom*, 284.

31. I am indebted to Ann Gillian Chu for her research paper on the debates my work has occasioned in Hong Kong about the place of the church in the Umbrella Movement. The full title of her work is "An Analysis of the Understanding of and Engagements with Stanley Hauerwas: Theological Convictions among Selected Hong Kong Theologians in Occupy Central and Umbrella Movements."

32. Michael Ignatieff, *The Ordinary Virtues: Moral Order in a Divided World* (Cambridge: Oxford University Press, 2017), 4.

33. Ignatieff, *The Ordinary Virtues*, 17.

34. Ignatieff, *The Ordinary Virtues*, 202–3.

9. Race

1. I am taking the liberty to edit the text in two ways—I have changed my use of the masculine pronoun, and rather than "black" or "negro," I have used "African American." There are some modes of writing that are too painful to repeat, even if you can claim that you did not know better. I do not think I knew better, but that may be self-deception. My general principle is that African Americans rightly tell white people how to refer to those who are not white. The difficulty is that no one description can do justice to the complexity of what it means to be white or black.

2. James Logan, "Liberalism, Race, and Stanley Hauerwas," *Cross Currents*, January 1, 2006, online. I wrote this article without having read Kristopher Norris's dissertation just written and defended in October 2017 at the University of Virginia entitled "Witnessing Whiteness: Hauerwas and Cone and the Challenge of Black Theology for Postliberal Ecclesiology." Norris's dissertation has a fair and quite critical account of my declaration that one of the reasons I have not written more on racial matters is that I have a different story than those stories that are determined by slavery and racism. Norris quotes Cone, who quite rightly says that cannot be true because no white person can fail to recognize our complicity with racism. I had disavowed writing on race because I worried that to do so as a white man, I would end up colonizing the African American story. But that does not mean that there were not ways I should have explored that make it possible to write on race. I highly commend Norris's work for no other reason than that he is able to identify conceptual moves Cone and I share, though it remains the case that we have very different ways of doing theology.

3. See, for example, my "Remembering Martin Luther King Jr. Remembering," in *Wilderness Wanderings: Probing Twentieth-Century Theology and Philosophy* (Boulder, CO: Westview, 1997), 225–38, and my "Why Time Cannot and Should Not Heal the Wounds of History, But Time Has Been and Can Be Redeemed," in *A Better Hope: Resources for a Church Confronting Capitalism, Democracy, and Postmodernity* (Grand Rapids, MI: Brazos, 2000), 139–54.

4. Jonathan Tran, "Time for Hauerwas's Racism," in *Unsettling Arguments: A Festschrift on the Occasion of Stanley Hauerwas's 70th Birthday,* ed. Charlie Collier, Charles Pinches, and Kelly Johnson (Eugene, OR: Cascade, 2010), 260.

5. I am indebted to Dr. Kristopher Norris for calling attention to my mistaken idea that I wrote the article in 1968. It was published on February 5, 1969, in the *Augustana Observer.* That I got the date wrong may not be all that important, but Kristopher Norris's dissertation is an extremely important critical account of James Cone and my work on race. Norris argues that in fact Cone and I share some fundamental concepts that could make us more in agreement than either

of us has thought. See Kristopher Norris, "Witnessing Whiteness: Hauerwas and Cone and the Challenge of Black Theology for Postliberal Ecclesiology" (Ph.D. diss., University of Virginia, 2017).

6. For my account of King and his commitment to nonviolence, see my chapter "Martin Luther King Jr. and Christian Nonviolence," in *War and the American Difference* (Grand Rapids, MI: Baker, 2011), 83–98.

7. For a strong defense of reparations, see Jennifer Harvey, *Dear White Christians: For Those Still Longing for Racial Reconciliation* (Grand Rapids, MI: Eerdmans, 2014). I think Harvey makes a strong case for reparations, but her account of reconciliation is far too shallow. Reparations and reconciliation are not necessarily in competition with one another.

8. Joseph Winters, *Hope Draped in Black: Race, Melancholy, and the Agony of Progress* (Durham, NC: Duke University Press, 2017), 15.

9. Winters, *Hope Draped in Black*, 42.

10. Winters, *Hope Draped in Black*, 210–21.

11. Winters, *Hope Draped in Black*, 190.

12. Winters, *Hope Draped in Black*, 191.

13. Reggie Williams, *Bonhoeffer's Black Jesus: Harlem Renaissance Theology and an Ethic of Resistance* (Waco, TX: Baylor University Press, 2014), 139.

14. For my account of Campbell, see my "Race: The 'More' It Is About: The Will Campbell Lecture," in my and Rom Coles's *Christianity, Democracy, and the Radical Ordinary* (Eugene, OR: Cascade, 2008), 87–102.

10. To Be Befriended

1. Brian Brock, *Wondrously Wounded: Theology, Disability, and the Body of Christ* (Waco, TX: Baylor University Press, 2019), 195.

2. Brock, *Wondrously Wounded*, xvi–xcvii.

3. For a more extended discussion of this observation, see my *Suffering Presence: Theological Reflections on Medicine, the Mentally Handicapped, and the Church* (Notre Dame, IN: University of Notre Dame Press, 1986), 173–75.

4. These remarks about fear I owe to a former student, Bruce McCuskey.

5. Hans Reinders, *Receiving the Gift of Friendship: Profound Disability, Theological Anthropology, and Ethics* (Grand Rapids, MI: Eerdmans, 2008), 313.

6. Brock, *Wondrously Wounded*, xiv.

7. Brock, *Wondrously Wounded*, xv.

8. I owe this way of putting the matter to my good friend Sam Wells.

9. Here I draw on David Hunsicker's use of O'Donovan to characterize Barth's significance in his *The Making of Stanley Hauerwas: Bridging Barth and Postliberalism* (Downers Grove, IL: Intervarsity Press [IVP], 2019), 72.

10. As much as I admire Brock's way of describing the intellectually disabled, it is hard to use Brock's revision in every context in which people with intellectual disabilities are described.

11. For my attempt to think through Sam Wells's account of what it means to "be with" someone applied to the mentally disabled, see my *Approaching the End: Eschatological Reflections on Church, Politics, and Life* (Grand Rapids, MI: Eerdmans, 2013), 222–36.

12. James McEvoy, "Friendship and Love," *Irish Theological Quarterly* 50, no. 1 (March 1, 1983): 45.

13. David Toole has directed my attention to Johnathan Lear's account of our vulnerability that is a manifestation of our nature as "finite erotic creatures." Accordingly, courage is and must be always included in accounts of the virtues because the very fragility of our lives requires it. Lear seems to be reading Freud through Plato—a remark that requires too much attention to be developed here. Lear develops these themes in his remarkable book *Radical Hope* (Cambridge, MA: Harvard University Press, 2006).

14. Patrick McKearney, "Receiving the Gift of Cognitive Disability: Recognizing Agency in the Limits of the Rational Subject," *Cambridge Anthropology* 36, no. 1 (Spring 2018): 40+; hereafter the online text is cited parenthetically in the chapter text.

15. Jonathan Tran pointed out to me that McKearney's "discovery" is quite similar to the argument Alice Crary develops in her book *Inside Ethics: On the Demands of Moral Thought* (Cambridge, MA: Harvard University Press, 2016). Crary argues that our moral lives depend on empirical discoverable qualities of human beings and animals (88). She suggests, therefore, that a certain exercise of the imagination is required in order to bring human beings and animals into focus in ethics.

16. Brock, *Wondrously Wounded*, 150–52.

17. Brock, *Wondrously Wounded*, 162–64.

18. Brock, *Wondrously Wounded*, 168.

19. Brock, *Wondrously Wounded*, 223.

20. Vanier, *Befriending the Stranger*, vii.

21. Jason Reimer Greig, *Reconsidering Intellectual Disability: L'Arche, Medical Ethics, and Christian Friendship* (Washington, DC: Georgetown University Press, 2015), 146.

22. Greig, *Reconsidering Intellectual Disability*, 226.

23. Jean Vanier, *Drawn into the Mystery of Jesus through the Gospel of John* (New York: Paulist Press, 2004), 231.

24. Vanier, *Drawn into the Mystery of Jesus*, 232.

25. Thomas Aquinas, *Summa theologica* (Westminster, MD: Christian Classics, 1981), I–II, 65, 5. For an account of Thomas on friendship, see Paul Wadell, *Friends of God: Virtues and Gifts in Aquinas* (New York: Peter Lang, 1991).

INDEX

SMH refers to Stanley Martin Hauerwas.

absolutism, 64, 66, 68, 75

acknowledgment as response required by knowledge, 176–77

Adams, Richard: *Watership Down,* 168, 174

adultery, 111

advice to Christian theologians, 165–70; choice of press for first publication, 166–67; criticism as necessary part of education and writing, 168; early church, required knowledge of, 168; friendship's important role, 168–69; future of theology, 169–70; reading widely, 167–69; Scripture, required knowledge of, 169, 172; writing as continuing education, 169; "writing in" vs. "writing out," 166, 174. *See also* writing

Aers, David, 43

African Americans. *See* race and racism

agape identified with utilitarianism, 111

agency, 82, 108, 122, 155, 157, 159

"all lives matter," 144

America: Christendom model in, 19, 125; identity and society of, 19; immigrants viewed with distrust in, 124; making America great again presumed to be recovery of (white) Christian America, 120; middle-class life in, 140; secular nature of church in, 19, 87; socially established religion of, 124; values of equality and achievement from Christian churches in, 87. *See also* race and racism

American Catholic Philosophical Association, 96

American exceptionalism, 148

Anabaptists, 18

anarchy: Church's stand against, 47–49; democracy's role and, 139

Anselm, 94, 98

anthropology: Barth's, 21–22, 37, 155; liberal theology and, 89; Niebuhr's anthropological method, 54, 75; pastoral care and naturalistic anthropology, 108

anti-Semitism, 12, 14

Apocalypse of John, 99

Apostles' Creed, 36

Aquinas, Thomas: as Aristotelian, 82; Barth and, 95; on God's desire to befriend us, 163, 192n25; MacIntyre and, 82–83, 85, 97–98, 184n5; natural theology and natural law of, 98; on relationship between philosophy and theology, 82–83; *Summa theologiae*, 82

Arche, l', communities, 152, 155–60, 162

Aristotle and Aristotelianism, 82, 84, 155

Asia, church in, 6, 117–34, 188n1; Christians in politics and, 117–18; cultural determinants, effect of, 119, 122; Ding Guangxun and, 125–29; as house church movement, 131; missionaries' history and, 122–23, 128; nationalism and, 125; recommendations for, 130–34; SMH's reception in Asia, 117–18; sustaining its mission throughout time, 131; Wang Mingdao and, 125–29

atheism, 91, 94, 96–97, 185n28

Augustana College (Rock Island, Illinois), 135, 143

Augustine, 30–32, 181n9; *The Confessions*, 172; MacIntyre and, 81, 85, 184n2

Austin, John, 86

autonomous individuals, 26

Ayer, Alfred Jules: *Language, Truth, and Logic*, 86

Balthasar, Hans Urs von, 88

Barmen Declaration (1934), 69–70, 74

Barth, Karl: analogies, use of, 46–49, 50, 52, 74; anthropology of, 21–22, 37, 155; as anti-American, 76; as apocalyptic theologian, 1; Aquinas and, 95; awareness of the world and, 9–10; Bildung tradition and, 2; Brock and, 155; casuistry of, 5; as champion of individuals at border of human life, 155; criticisms of, 10–11, 24, 40, 73–74, 88; differences with Niebuhr, 54, 64–80; "found" sentences and, 24; as fundamentalist, 66; on God, 4, 5, 12, 36–37, 43–44, 68, 95; "honest ignorance" of, 125, 129, 130–31; on justice, 10, 72, 79; on liberal theology, 4, 66, 79, 110; MacIntyre and, 88–89; Mozart as love of, 112; pastoral care and, 112–16; as pastoral theologian, 6, 112; pessimism of, 67; providence, account of, 3; radical theological perspective of, 1–2; response to Brunner's criticism, 77–78; Romans commentary and, 43–45, 64–66, 89; SMH working in spirit of, 4–5; theocentric theology of, 24–25; theological politics of, 3; Wittgenstein and, 28, 34–35, 88. *See also* Christology; humanism; Nazis and Adolf Hitler; Niebuhr, Reinhold; Russian Communism

Barth, Karl, works by: *Against the Stream: Shorter Post-War Writings, 1946–1952*, 3, 10–11, 18, 22, 24–25, 40, 41, 77, 180n6, 182n7; *Anselm: Fides Quaerens Intellectum*, 95; Bernese Pastors' Association, letter to, 15; "The Christian Community and the Civil Community," 40, 41, 74; "The Christian Community in the Midst of Political Change," 41; "The Christian Message and the New Humanism" (lecture 1949), 24–25; "The Christian Message in Europe Today," 13–14; "Church and State," 43, 74, 181n3; *Church Dogmatics*, 3, 27–28, 35, 37, 182n7; *Community,*

State, and Church, 40, 43; *Dogmatics in Outline*, 35–36; *God in Action*, 113; "Gospel and Law," 74, 181n3; "Hermeneutics of Providence: Theology, Race, and Divine Action in History" (dissertation), 13; *The Humanity of God*, 3; *Protestant Thought: From Rousseau to Ritschl*, 2

Bede, 121, 127

Beeley, Christopher: *Leading God's People: Wisdom from the Early Church for Today*, 104

Bildung tradition, 2

Black Lives Matter, 144

Black Power movement, 7, 137–43, 144

Boisen, Anton, 105

Bonhoeffer, Dietrich, 51, 149, 182n8

Book of Common Prayer, 114–15

Borradori, Giovanna, 84, 88

Brock, Adam, 160–61

Brock, Brian: *Beginnings: Interrogating Hauerwas* (with SMH), 168, 173, 176–77; *Wondrously Wounded: Theology, Disability, and the Body of Christ*, 153–55, 160, 191n10

Brown, Peter: *Western Christendom*, 121

Brunner, Emil, 11; "An Open Letter" to Barth, 11, 13, 76–78

Bultmann, Rudolph, 89, 90, 92

Bush, Eberhard, 70

Campbell, Will, 149

Cao, Nanlai, 189n17

capitalism, 20, 90, 109

Carnegie Centennial Project, 132

casuistry, 5, 6

Cavell, Stanley, 28, 29, 33–34, 176–77; *The Claim of Reason: Wittgenstein, Skepticism, Morality, and Tragedy*, 32–33

Center for Ethics and Culture at Notre Dame conference (April 2014), 83

charity, 83, 163

China and Three-Self Movement, 126–28, 189n17, 189n19

Christ. *See* Jesus Christ

Christian Century, twentieth century as, 19–20

Christian Family Movement, 166

Christian identity vs. European identity, 4

Christian values and ethics: allowing people to live peaceably, 132; Niebuhr's critique of Barth and, 67; Niebuhr's social ethics, 63, 68; situations ethics, 111; social order suffused with, 21

Christology: Barth's analogies and, 50–51, 74; freedom of church and, 18; misunderstanding of Barth's, 21; Niebuhr on Barth's, 66, 74–75; Niebuhr's, 56, 59; SMH's work and, 51; the state in the New Testament and, 44

Chu, Ann Gillian, 189n31

Church of the Holy Family (Chapel Hill, North Carolina), 100

church's role: call for church to reclaim its visibility, 42; as Constantinian church, 45; ecumenical, 48; as ministry of the congregation, 48; prophetic, 104; state church vs. free church, 42; sustained by courage from work of the Holy Spirit, 114; telling the truth and keeping the state in check, 52; "to be the church," 18, 41, 42–43, 125, 129; "to make the world the world," 18, 39, 49–51, 102. *See also* pastoral care

Cioffi, Todd, 51

civil rights movement, 140, 145, 148–49

Civil War, U.S., 144, 146

class, issues of, 136. *See also* the poor

classical humanism, 25, 27

Clebsch, William: *Pastoral Care in Historical Perspective* (with Jackle), 106–7

clergy's role. *See* pastoral care
Coakley, Sarah, 105
Cold War, 76
commentary tradition of writing, 172–73
common way of life across Christendom, 121–22
Communism. *See* Russian Communism
Cone, James, 190n2, 190n5
Continental theology, 73
continuing education of theologians, 169
conversation, theology as, 176–77
courage, 114, 192n13
COVID-19 pandemic: as apocalyptic moment, 1; easy to lose track of time and to despair during, 7
Crary, Alice, 192n15
Curry, Michael, 119

Dante, 168
Darwin, Charles, 54–55
Das, Veena, 159
Dean, Robert: *For the Life of the World: Jesus Christ and the Church in the Theologies of Dietrich Bonhoeffer and Stanley Hauerwas,* 51
democracy, 19, 39, 49–51, 62, 133, 138–39
Descartes, René, 113
despair, 22, 133
detective fiction, 61
Dewey, John, 59
Ding Guangxun, 125–29
dissertations, choice of topic for, 166
Dorrien, Gary, 72
Dostoevsky, Fyodor, 97
Du Bois, W. E. B.: *The Souls of Black Folks,* 147
dying, care for the, 104
dying Christendom. *See* end of Christendom

Eastern Europe, Barth's position on Communist regimes in, 70, 76, 128–29
East Germany, 128–29
emotivism, culture of, 108

end of Christendom, 19–20, 23, 41; in Global South, 20; recovering theological voice in, 38, 102, 120; retreat of Christianity due to anticolonialism and, 123; survival of the church, 22; in the West, 118
English Christendom, 121
Enlightenment, 26, 106
Ephesians 2:11–21, 119
ethics. *See* Christian values and ethics
Eucharist, 115
Europe: Christian identity vs. European identity, 4, 19; Christian revival, possibility of, 15–16; freeing church from its European captivity, 18–22; nihilism's effect in, 14; postwar ability to sustain joy and patience in, 18; postwar choice between America or Russia, 15; theological heresy at heart of Christianity in, 13–14; "we" of Barth used to mean, 18–19
evangelism, 22
Evans, G. R.: *A History of Pastoral Care,* 106
evil, 86, 97

feminism, 7
Feuerbach, Ludwig, 54, 92
Fides et ratio (encyclical), 85, 184–85n12
Fides Press, 166
Fleming, Richard, 29
Fletcher, Joseph, 111
foot washing, 162
forgiveness: as everyday virtue, 133; reconciliation with those harmed by those forgiven, 150; of sin, relationship to healing, 112–14
freedom: of the church, 18–22, 44, 79, 129; in modernity, 109; in political realm, 47–48, 142
free will, 26
Freud, Sigmund, 192n13
friendships: communal nature of, 153; importance in doing theological

task, 168–69; with intellectually disabled persons, 152–64. *See also* intellectually disabled persons, friendships with

Genesis, 99

Geuss, Raymond: *A World without Why*, 55

Gilkey, Langdon, 57–59; *On Niebuhr: A Theological Study*, 57

globalization, 132, 188n6

Global South's end of Christendom, 20

God: anger of, 48–49; Barth on, 4, 5, 12, 36–37, 43–44, 68, 95; Christian doctrine of, 98; duty of humans to obey, 45; existence of, 85, 93–98, 113; history, presence in, 17; humanism of, 3, 25–26; MacIntyre on, 95–99; Niebuhr on, 54; as One for Jews, Christians, and Muslims, 93; Protestant liberals' view of, 25. *See also* theism; theocentric theology of Barth

"God is God," 4, 22, 24, 175

God's kingdom, 71, 129–30

Goethe, Johann Wolfgang von, 2

Gonzalez, Justo, 19–20

Gorringe, Timothy, 181n6

grace of God, 17, 18, 26, 129, 175, 180n5

Great Depression, 58

Greece as home of Western philosophy, 120

Greig, Jason Reimer: *Reconsidering Intellectual Disability: L'Arche, Medical Ethics, and Christian Friendship*, 162

guilt of white liberals, 142

Hall, Douglas John, 20

Hargaden, Kevin, 176, 177

Harvey, Jennifer, 191n7

Harvey, Thomas Alan, 189n20

Hauerwas, Stanley Martin (SMH): as anti-Christendom theologian, 121; at Augustana College, 135, 143; career success as theologian, 165–66; criticism of, 5, 39–40, 51, 136, 190n2; as godfather of Adam Brock, 160; Hong Kong, debate over SMH's place in Umbrella Movement in, 132, 189n31; memoir by, 172; at Notre Dame, 164; in pastoral role, 101; reasons for publishing his works, 166, 175; as sectarian, 120; sharing Barth's view of liberal theology, 4–5

Hauerwas, Stanley Martin, works by: *Approaching the End: Eschatological Reflections on Church, Politics, and Life*, 192n11; *Beginnings: Interrogating Hauerwas* (with Brock), 168, 173, 176–77; *The Character of Virtue: Letters to a Godson*, 176; *Conversation* (with Wells), 168; *Cross-Shattered Christ: Meditations on the Seven Last Words*, 175; "An Ethical Appraisal of Black Power," 7, 135, 137–43, 190n1; *Fully Alive*, 2; *Lord Teach Us*, 175; *Matthew*, 173, 175; *Performing the Faith: Bonhoeffer and the Practice of Nonviolence*, 182n8; *Prayers Plain Spoken*, 176; *Resident Aliens: Life in the Christian Colony* (with Willimon) (foreword for Japanese translation), 118–19, 175; *Suffering Presence: Theological Reflections on Medicine, the Mentally Handicapped, and the Church*, 191n3; *The Truth about God: The Ten Commandments in Christian Life* (with Willimon), 175; *Vision and Virtue*, 166, 174; *With the Grain of the Universe: The Church's Witness and Natural Theology*, 4, 27, 51, 53, 55, 62, 187n49

Hegel, Georg Wilhelm Friedrich, 2, 9, 11, 60

Heidegger, Martin, 27, 92

hell and purgatory, 92

Hepburn, Ronald, 86

Herberg, Will, 40, 74, 180n5

Herder, Johann Gottfried von, 2

Herdt, Jennifer, 23; *Forming Humanity: Redeeming the German Bildung Tradition*, 2

Heschel, Abraham, 61–62

historical method in writing, 173

history, God's presence in, 17

Hitler, Adolf. *See* Nazis and Adolf Hitler

Holy Roman Empire, 14

Hong Kong, debate over Umbrella Movement in, 132, 189n31

hope: in a hopeless world, 22; liberalism's effect on, 90; progress as condition of, 147; sustaining in face of death, 92; truth making hope possible in face of injustice, 151

Horton, Douglas: translation of *Word of God and Theology* by, 65

Hough, Joseph: *Black Power and White Protestants*, 139

humanism, 1–3; in Barth's *Against the Stream*, 3, 24–26; Barth's doctrine of God and, 25–26; classical, 25, 27; label of antihumanistic applied to Barth, 4; language of theology and, 37–38; love of all things human and, 115; relevant to today's world, 1–2; theocentric, 27, 38

human life, narrative coherence of, 98–99

human rights discourse, 132–33

Humboldt, Wilhelm von, 2

humor, 17, 45, 176

Hungary's subjugation by Soviets, 10, 76–79

Hunsicker, David: *The Making of Stanley Hauerwas: Bridging Barth and Postliberalism*, 4–5, 6, 191n9

Hunsinger, Deborah: *Theology and Pastoral Counseling: A New Interdisciplinary Approach*, 112–13

Hunsinger, George, 41, 74–75

Ignatieff, Michael: *The Ordinary Virtues: Moral Order in a Divided World*, 132–33

illiteracy of Christians for most of Christian history, 171

immigrants in American society, 124

injustice: Niebuhr on man's inclination to, 62; slavery and, 144; truth making hope possible in face of, 151

insight, 24, 59–63

intellectually disabled persons, friendships with, 152–64; Adam Brock's witness, 160–61; agency from acknowledgment of vulnerability, 157–58; caring for intellectually disabled persons making the caregiver a better person, 154; descriptions of intellectually disabled persons, 153, 191n10; fear as element in, 153, 163–64, 191n4; freedom from judgment and spontaneity of mentally disabled, 159; Jesus commanding us to be befriended by the weak, the needy, and the lonely, 163; McEvoy on, 156, 163; McKearney on, 156–60, 163; mental disabilities enabling ethical interactions, 159–60; shared vulnerability of all people, 156, 158; sharing a common world, 157–58, 163; Singer on, 156; unequal power relation between mentally disabled and caregiver, 155; Vanier and, 161–63

interrogations as form of writing, 173

Jackle, Charles: *Pastoral Care in Historical Perspective* (with Clebsch), 106–7

James, William, 53–55; *The Will to Believe*, 55

Jantzen, Matt: "Hermeneutics of Providence: Theology, Race, and Divine Action in History," 3, 13–14, 17, 180n6, 182n7

Japanese Christians, 118–19. *See also* Asia, church in

jargon in theological writing, 173

Jesus Christ: as actuality of the Christian message, 25; demythologizing of gospel of, 92; Europe's need to proclaim anew his eternal truth, 17; healing of the paralytic, 113; humanism and, 4, 26, 47; identity of, 26; in pastoral care we offer one another, 115–16; resurrection of, 26; truth and, 36; Wright's depiction of, 83

Jews, 93, 119

Jim Crow laws, 146

justice: Barth's understanding of, 10; between-wars generation and, 58; Niebuhr on Barth's irresponsibility in relation to, 72, 79; Niebuhr on man's capacity for, 62; race and, 138–39, 146

Kant, Immanuel, 2, 133

Kaye, Bruce, 127, 130–31; *The Rise and Fall of English Christendom: Theocracy, Christology, Order and Power,* 121–22

Kelsey, David: *Beyond Athens and Berlin,* 105

Kerr, Fergus, 186n48

King, Martin Luther, Jr., 140, 145

Kittay, Eva, 156

Kuyper, Abraham, 126

language: of Christians, 21; "found" sentences and, 23–24; ordinary language philosophy, 27–34; of theology, 34–38

Lap Yan Kung, 188n2

Last Judgment, 98

law, role of, 47

Lear, Johnathan, 192n13

Leithart, Peter: *The End of Protestantism: Pursuing Unity in a Fragmented Church,* 123–24

Levellers, 185n17

liberal theology: Barth's criticism of, 4, 66, 79, 110; language of theology and, 34–35; MacIntyre's criticism of, 88–92; Niebuhr and, 56; SMH's sharing Barth's view of, 4–5

literary criticism, 177

local character of Christian formations, 121–22, 125

Logan, James, 136

Lonergan, Bernard, 60–61; *Insight,* 24

Long, Steve, 186n38

Lord's Prayer, 175

love: God's love manifested in human existence, 26; of other beings, 17; pastoral care and, 111

luck, 110

lust, 62

Lutheran dualism, 70, 74

MacIntyre, Alasdair, 6, 81–99; on alienation from Christianity, 88; Aquinas and, 82–83, 85, 97–98, 184n5; as Augustinian Christian, 81; Barth and, 88–89; on belief and Christianity, 85–88; critique of liberal theology by, 88–92; interview with Borradori, 84, 88; Marxism and, 87, 89–90; as philosopher, 81, 90, 99; on psychological theories that inform pastoral care, 109; on relationship between theology and philosophy, 82–85, 184n10, 184–85n12; Riddel Memorial Lectures (University of Newcastle 1967), 90–91; as Roman Catholic, 81–83, 86, 93–95, 184n2; as social conservative, 6; Thomism and, 82–83; Wittgenstein and, 86, 88, 186n48

MacIntyre, Alasdair, works by: "Address Delivered at the Inauguration of Paul Joseph Philibert, O.P. as President of the Dominican School of Philosophy and Theology in 1987," 98, 186n48; *After Virtue,* 82, 108; "Catholic Instead of What?," 83; *Ethics in the Conflicts of Modernity: An Essay on Desire, Practical Reasoning, and Narrative,* 95, 109; *God, Philosophy, Universities: A Selective*

MacIntyre, Alasdair, works by (*continued*)
History of the Catholic Philosophical Tradition, 84, 93, 95–96; "Intractable Moral Disagreements," 97–98; "Is Understanding Religion Compatible with Believing?," 87; *Marxism and Christianity* (introduction, 1995 ed.), 88; "Marxists and Christians," 185n17; *Metaphysical Beliefs* (preface by MacIntyre, 1970 ed.), 86, 88; "Natural Law as Subversive: The Case of Aquinas," 98; "On Being a Theistic Philosopher in a Secularized Culture," 96; *The Religious Significance of Atheism* (with Ricoeur), 91; *Secularization and Moral Change,* 90, 92; "Three Kinds of Atheism," 94, 185n28; *Three Rival Versions of Moral Enquiry: Encyclopedia, Genealogy, and Tradition,* 86; "Truth as a Good: A Reflection on *Fides et Ratio,*" 184–85n12; "What Has Christianity to Say to the Moral Philosopher?," 83; *Whose Justice? Which Rationality?,* 81, 184n2
Mahn, Jason: *Becoming a Christian in Christendom: Radical Discipleship and the Way of the Cross in America's "Christian" Culture,* 20–22
Maimonides, 186n46
Marquardt, Friedrich-Wilhelm, 40–41
Marxism, 87, 89–90, 185n17
Matthew, SMH's commentary on, 173, 175
May, Bill, 166
McCabe, Herbert, 186n48
McCuskey, Bruce, 191n4
McEvoy, James, 156, 163
McInerny, Ralph, 81
McKearney, Patrick: "Receiving the Gift of Cognitive Disability: Recognizing Agency in the Limits of the Rational Subject," 156–60, 163, 192n15
melancholy, 147
Mennonites, 122

mentally disabled persons, friendships with. *See* intellectually disabled persons, friendships with
mercy of God, 43, 48–49
Methodism, 21–22
Methodist Youth Fellowship (MYF), 101
Middle Ages, 107
missionaries, 122–23, 128
modernity, 26, 89, 91, 108–9
Moi, Toril, 27–34; *Revolution of the Ordinary: Literary Studies after Wittgenstein, Austin, and Cavell,* 28–29, 176–77
morality: America's race question and, 136–46; Europe and, 14; Gilkey on, 57–59; globalization and, 132; MacIntyre on, 88, 97–98, 184n2, 184n5; mentally disabled as moral agents, 156–60; in Middle Ages, 107; of modernity, 41, 108–9; Niebuhr on, 57–59, 67–68; pastoral care and, 111; societal, 87. *See also* Christian values and ethics
Morgan, Brandon: "The Lordship of Christ and the Gathering of the Church: Hauerwas's Debt to the 1948 Barth–Niebuhr Exchange," 79
Mozart, Barth's love of, 112
Murdoch, Iris, 166, 174
Muslims, 93

narcissism, 102, 110
nationalism, rise of, 125
National Socialism of Germany. *See* Nazis and Adolf Hitler
natural law, 10, 45, 46, 97–98
natural theology, 62, 95, 97, 98
nature, 175
Nazis and Adolf Hitler, 3, 11–15, 37; Barth's condemnation of, 10, 11–13, 40, 44, 48, 69, 77–78, 129; as false manifestation of "religion," 12, 69, 77; "post-Christian" terminology of, 71
neo-orthodox theologians, 71
Newman, J. H., 95, 96

Niebuhr, H. Richard: *The Purpose of the Church and Its Ministry,* 108

Niebuhr, Reinhold, 5–6, 39, 53–63; on Barth, 10–11, 40, 64–65; Bonn meeting with Barth, 65; character of, 63; Communism, in opposition to, 76; differences with Barth, 54, 64–80; Gilkey and, 57–59; importance of insights of, 59–63; intellectual aspects of faith interwoven with ethics for, 67; intelligence of, 63; as Jamesian, 54–55; relationship with Barth, 6, 180n3; SMH influenced by, 149; SMH's criticism of and regard for, 53, 56, 63; social gospel and, 39, 181n1

Niebuhr, Reinhold, works by: "Barth—Apostle of the Absolute," 65; "Barthianism and Political Reaction," 68; "Barthianism and the Kingdom," 68; *Beyond Tragedy: Essays on the Christian Interpretation of Tragedy,* 60; *The Children of Light and the Children of Darkness,* 62; "Karl Barth on Politics," 69; *The Nature and Destiny of Man,* 62; "Transvaluation of Values," 60; "We Are Men and Not God," 72; "Why Is Barth Silent on Hungary?," 77, 79

Nietzsche, Friedrich Wilhelm, 21, 92, 185n28

nihilism, 12, 14, 42, 144

Noahide code, 186n46

Norris, Kristopher, 190n2, 190n5

Novak, David, 186n46

Noyce, Gay, 101–2

Nussbaum, Martha, 81, 184n2

Obama, Barack, 145; "A More Perfect Union" speech (March 2008), 148

Occupy Central Movement, 132

O'Donovan, Joan, 155, 191n9

Olympic Games (1936), 15

original sin, 184n2

orthodox Christianity, 92, 93

Pabst, Adrian, 109

pacifism, 57, 72

parables in New Testament, 35

pastoral care, 6, 100–116; American version vs. theological tradition, 111; asking for help, 103–4; avoiding being judgmental, 110; Barth and, 112–16; basic functions of, 107; care for the dying, 104; clinical pastoral education (CPE), 105, 187n4; contemporary understanding of, 108–12; counseling and, 110; deep humanity required of agents of care, 115; as expression of work of the Holy Spirit, 114; history of care that Christians give one another, 105–8; importance for upbuilding of the church, 103–5; ministry as a helping profession, 102–3; psychological theories that inform, 109; secular caring as part of, 111; as separate discipline without theological warrant, 110–11; as work of the whole church, 100–101, 114

Pattison, Stephen, 111

philosophy: Greece as home of Western philosophy, 120; ordinary language, 27–34; relationship with theology, 82–85, 184n10, 184–85n12

physics, 97

Plato, 120, 192n13

political character of the church, 11, 40, 45

political history, 11

political theology, 3–4, 39–43, 49, 50, 74

politics: Barth's interest in and judgments on, 41, 72, 75, 78, 129, 132; Black Power movement and, 140–41; pastoral care informed by liberal political theory and practice, 109; search for identity and, 141; separate from theology, 41, 69, 77; separate functions of legislative, executive, and judicial, 48

Pontius Pilate, 43

poor: importance of helping, 47; rights discourse and, 133

post-Christian era, 71. *See also* end of Christendom

postliberalism, 5

pragmatism, 54–55, 78

prayer, 83, 94, 176

pride, 60, 62, 68

prophets, 61–62

proselytizing and attracting new members to the church, 21

Protestantism, 6, 114, 124–25

Protestant liberalism, 5, 21, 25, 89, 92, 110. *See also* liberal theology

Psalms, 104

purity of the faith, 75

race and racism, 7, 135–51; African American belief in God, 122; Americans dealing with, 123, 146–47; attempt of white America to relegate slavery to "history," 144; Black Lives Matter, 144; Black Power movement, 7, 137–43, 144; Bonhoeffer on, 149–50; as central challenge to America's morality, 136; class issues inherent in, 136; democracy and, 138–39; economic character of, 146; failure of civil rights movement's success and, 145, 148–49; guilt of white liberals, 142; Hauerwas's article: "An Ethical Appraisal of Black Power," 7, 135, 137–43, 190n1; inadequacy of good intentions and, 138, 139; integration vs. reverse segregation, 137; Jim Crow laws, 146; justice and equality in terms of, 138–39; melancholy of telling African American story, 147; middle-class life in America and, 140; presumption that race is problem for African Americans, 136; prevalence of racism in American life, 145; progress as way of forgetting, 147–48; reconciliation and,

137–38; reparations, 146, 191n7; salvation and, 150; search for identity and, 141–42; sin of racism, 149–50; Trump's presidency and, 149; visibility of everyday brutality of, 144, 146

realism, 31, 57, 59

reconciliation, 110, 113, 133; race and, 137–38, 150, 191n7

Reformation, 70, 106, 128

Reformational Catholicism, 124

Reinders, Hans: *Receiving the Gift of Friendship: Profound Disability, Theological Anthropology, and Ethics,* 153–54

relativism, 66–67

religious perfectionism, 68

Religious Right, 22

resilience, 133

revelation, 66, 113

Ricoeur, Paul: *The Religious Significance of Atheism* (with MacIntyre), 91

rights discourse, 132–33

right words and actions, 18

Robert, Dana, 123

Robinson, John, 89

Roman Catholics: actuality of the Christian message for, 25; MacIntyre and, 81–83, 86, 93–95, 184n2; salvation and, 118

Romans 13: Barth's commentary and, 43–45, 64–66, 89; Three-Self Movement and, 127

Russell, Bertrand, 59

Russian Communism, 3, 11–13; Barth's opinion on, 10–12, 40, 76–77, 180n5; as imperialism in new form, 15; Niebuhr on Barth's response to, 77–79

Sacks, Jonathan, 186n46

salvation, 22, 73, 118, 119, 150

Santayana, George, 59

Sartre, Jean-Paul, 27, 79

Schiller, Friedrich, 2

Schleiermacher, Friedrich Daniel Ernst, 90, 105
secularism: increase of, related to language of rights, 132–33; MacIntyre and, 84, 87–88, 89, 91, 97; nature of church in America and, 19, 21, 87; pastoral care including secular caring, 111
sensuality, 62
sermons, 171–73, 175
Shakespeare, William: *King Lear,* 34
sin, 27, 60, 62, 67, 75, 107, 184n2; forgiveness of, 112–14; racism as, 149–50
Singer, Peter, 156–57, 160
situations ethics, 111
skepticism, 30, 34, 42, 52, 87
slavery, 144–50
Smith, Ronald Gregor, 10
social ethics, 63, 68, 80
social gospel, 39, 181n1
socialism, 68, 89–90
social justice, 68
social progress, Barth's criticism of, 67
Starr, Chloe: *Chinese Theology: Text and Context,* 125–29
state, the: Barth's analogies and, 46–49; church's telling of truth as check on, 52; concept of, 42–46; secrecy and tyranny of, 47, 48
suffering, 154
Sumner, George, 187n1
systematic theology, 9, 35–36, 179–80n1

technical progress, spread of, 133
Ten Commandments, 175
theism, 91–97
theocentric humanism, 27, 38
theocentric theology of Barth, 24–25
Thomism, 82
Three-Self Movement, 126–28, 189n17, 189n19
Tillich, Paul: illumination of human experience by, 110; MacIntyre on, 90–92; pastoral theology and, 6; secularism and, 89; *Systematic Theology,* 35

tolerance, 133
Toole, David, 192n13
totalitarianism, 10–12, 76, 78. *See also* Nazis and Adolf Hitler; Russian Communism
Toulmin, Stephen, 86
Tran, Jonathan, 23, 35, 136, 192n15
Trinity, 120
Troeltsch, Ernst, 87, 90
Trump, Donald, 149
trust, 133
truth, 36, 52, 113, 126, 151
Tsang, Sam, 188n2

Umbrella Movement, 132, 189n31
unchurched, the, 21
University of Notre Dame, 164
university study of theology, 165
utilitarianism, 111

Vanier, Jean, 7, 155, 157, 161–63; *Befriending the Stranger,* 152
vulnerability of all people, 156–57

Wang Mingdao, 125–29, 189n20
war and violence, 49, 52, 57, 123–24, 130, 139
Wells, Sam, 23, 191n8, 192n11; *Conversation* (with SMH), 168; *Incarnational Ministry: Being with the Church,* 103
Wesley, John, 21
West, Charles, 180n5
Williams, Reggie: *Bonhoeffer's Black Jesus: Harlem Renaissance Theology and an Ethic of Resistance,* 149, 150
Williams, Rowan, 166
Willimon, Will: *Pastor: The Theology and Practice of Ordained Ministry,* 187n4; *Resident Aliens: Life in the Christian Colony* (with SMH), 118–19, 175; *The Truth about God: The Ten Commandments in Christian Life* (with SMH), 175

Winters, Joe: *Hope Draped in Black: Race, Melancholy, and the Agony of Progress,* 147–48

Wittgenstein, Ludwig, 27–35, 37, 55, 159, 174, 181n9; *Culture and Value,* 52; MacIntyre and, 86, 88, 186n48; *Philosophical Investigations,* 29–31

Woodword-Lehman, Darek, 179n6

World Council of Churches (WCC) meeting (Amsterdam 1948), 64–65, 67, 70–76; Barth's response to Niebuhr, 73–74; Niebuhr's response to Barth's speech at, 72–73, 75; theme of "Man's Disorder and God's Design," 70–71

worldview and "to make the world the world," 18, 39, 49–51, 102

World War I: church as witness to, 41; creation of sense of tragedy by, 67

World War II: church as witness to, 41; Niebuhr's writing upon end of, 62–63. *See also* Europe *for post-war years;* Nazis and Adolf Hitler

Wright, Jeremiah, 148

Wright, N. T., 83, 85

writing, 171–77; choice of genre, 172–73; choice of press for first publication, 166–67; commentary tradition, 172–73; as continuing education, 169; conversation, theology as, 176–77; criticism as necessary part of, 168; historical method in, 173; illiteracy of Christians for most of Christian history, 171; interrogations as form of, 173; jargon, 173; language, importance of, 174–75; literacy criticism, 177; memoirs, 172; mixing types of material in a book, 174; narrative, Christian theology as, 177; poetic effects in, 175–76; popular vs. scholarly theology, 174; as "remarks" in a collection of essays, 175; scholarly articles and monographs, 173–74; sermons, 171–73, 175; Wittgenstein's advice on, 174; "writing in" vs. "writing out," 166, 174

Yoder, John Howard, 40

young, responsibility of the, 41–42

Zhao, Wenjuan, 188n2

Richard E. Myers Lectures

More Things in Heaven and Earth: The Intertextuality of Shakespeare with Theology
PAUL S. FIDDES

Making the World Over: Confronting Racism, Misogyny, and Xenophobia in U.S. History
R. MARIE GRIFFITH